HE IS . . . I SAY

ALSO BY DAVID WILD

And the Grammy Goes To . . .: The Official Story of Music's Most Coveted Award

The Showrunners: A Season Inside the Billion-Dollar, Death-Defying, Madcap World of Television's Real Stars

Friends . . . 'til the End: The One with All Ten Years

HE IS . . . I SAY

How I Learned to Stop Worrying
and Love Neil Diamond

DAVID WILD

Da Capo Press
A Member of the Perseus Books Group

Cataloging-in-Publication data for this book is available from the Library of Congress.
First Da Capo Press edition 2008
ISBN 978-0-306-81784-7

Text design by *BackStory Design*

Published by Da Capo Press
A Member of the Perseus Books Group
http://www.dacapopress.com

Da Capo Press books are available at special discounts for bulk purchases in the U.S. by corporations, institutions, and other organizations. For more information, please contact the Special Markets Department at the Perseus Books Group, 2300 Chestnut Street, Suite 200, Philadelphia, PA 19103, or call (800) 810-4145, ext. 5000, or e-mail special.markets@perseusbooks.com.

1 2 3 4 5 6 7 8 9

A NOTE ON SOURCES
Unless noted otherwise, quotes come from the author's own interviews for *Rolling Stone, Behind the Music*, assorted Neil Diamond liner notes, and other projects.

Neil Diamond's lyrics are used by permission of The Diamond Music Companies, including DiamondSongs (SESAC), Prophet Music (SESAC), Stonebridge Music (SESAC) and Tallyrand Music (SESAC).

A complete list of song credits can be found on page 205.

CONTENTS

For my father, Stanley, my mother, Carol, my brother, Jeffrey, and my sister, Wendy, with whom I sang from the backseat.

And for my wife, Fran, and my sons, Andrew and Alec, with whom I sing now from the front seat.

Here's to all that beautiful noise.

Good times never seemed so good. My beloved brother Jeff and sister-in-law Susan are on the left. My lovely mother Carol and I are on the right. And if you don't recognize the man in the middle, then you are probably reading the wrong book. *(Courtesy Carol Wild)*

Coming to America,
More Specifically North Jersey

> Far we've been traveling far
> Without a home, but not without a star
> Free, only want to be free
> We huddle close, hang on to a dream
>
> – "AMERICA," BY NEIL DIAMOND

"Mr. Diamond would like to see you, Mrs. Wild."

The dreamy invitation for my mother to enjoy a personal audience with Neil Diamond—our own King of Kings, our Jewish American Elvis—arrived not from an angel on high, but from a large, formally dressed, middle-aged security man who carried himself with the impressive, monotone self-seriousness of a Secret Service operative. It was the fall of 1988, and in only a matter of moments the night's big Neil Diamond concert was scheduled to start before a sold-out crowd of more than twenty thousand, at the then Brendan Byrne Arena in East Rutherford, New Jersey—a grand Garden State gathering place that would later become the Continental Airlines Arena, and then, perhaps most fashionably of all, the Izod Center.

Scanning the rest of our small concert-going party—my older brother, Jeff, his wife, Susan, and myself—and doing a quick threat assessment, the security man then added, "Will you all follow me . . . *now,*" as he firmly motioned for us to hurry up and come along. The simple fact that this oversized fellow knew exactly in which seats to find the Wild party was enough to convince us that he was a properly authorized representative of all that is good in the universe—namely, Neil Diamond—rather than some nefarious figure curiously bent on leading us out of the Byrne Arena so that we would miss the Man's impending show. Frankly, when somebody hands you the Garden State—the reformed-Jew equivalent of a backstage pass to the Vatican— your first instinct isn't to look too terribly hard for any reasons to say no.

So it was with a collective sense of urgency that we did *exactly* as we were told, dutifully abandoning our choice floor seats as we followed this polite and possibly armed man down a hall, past a security check-point at which we were ceremoniously presented our priceless "All Access" stickers, then through a maze of backstage pre-show buzz. At long last, we reached the door of an unmarked room outside of which an even more intimidating security man stood guard, bravely placing himself in harm's way as the last wall of defense between the Man Who Would Be Diamond and our potentially lethal clan of shorter-than-average, mostly pudgy Jews.

Understandably, we were not privy to the next few moments of whispered, coded, and official-sounding conversations. Then finally and thankfully—after a series of very professional-sounding walkie-talkie transmissions and a supersecret pattern of knocks—the door in front of us opened and we were ushered in past what looked very much like the Gates of Heaven, at least if you happen to be someone who actually liked Neil Diamond's performance in *The Jazz Singer*.

And so while the rest of Diamond's flock faithfully waited in their seats just a few hundred yards and yet a million miles away, we alone were now being welcomed straight into the belly of the beast—the inner sanctum of the Frog King himself, Neil Diamond. For anyone with a lifelong sweet tooth for "Cherry, Cherry" or "Crunchy Granola Suite," this moment in time truly was as good as it gets.

For as long as I can remember, Neil Diamond had been one of the more consistently appealing presences inside the Wild home at 25 Glenwood Road in Tenafly, New Jersey, an affluent New York City suburb whose population was even more white than Diamond's live audience. To be fair, for five glorious, irony-rich weeks in 1973 when I was twelve and suddenly concerned about the racial imbalance of my hometown, NBC broadcast a drama series about a black private eye called, of all things, *Tenafly*. Legend had it that some Hollywood hotshot was driving down Route 9W in Bergen County, spotted an exit sign in the corner of his eye, and somehow thought that the town's name had some of the urban cool of *Superfly*.

This Hollywood hotshot thought wrong. *Tenafly* wasn't a big hit show, not even in Tenafly.

Neil Diamond, as I can personally attest, was big in Jersey well before Bruce Springsteen became The Boss. In our home in particular, his music was always near the very top of our pops. Coming of age in the early seventies in a sort of Dark Ages after the breakup of the Beatles and before the rise of disco, the music of Neil Diamond took a central place both in our eight-track tape players and in our hearts and minds. Through his indelible and almost absurdly infectious songs, Diamond unknowingly provided the brooding yet beautiful sound track for the good, the bad, and the ugly of our messy Wild life. Heard most often in the full aural glamour of the sound systems of boxy station wagons that my mother drove, Diamond's passionate and poppy music spoke to us—and to me in particular.

Through good times and even not-so-good times, Diamond offered suburban listeners like us the uplifting and radiant hope of "Sweet Caroline," for whom "good times never seemed so good."

Whether or not anyone in our house was actually scoring at any given time, Diamond brought the courtly romance in "Play Me," the sexy zest for life of "Cracklin' Rose," and the exotic, Afro-tinged sensuality of "Soolaimon." In lieu of any more orthodox religious belief, we even looked to Diamond for the answers to life's bigger questions. And unlike any of the religious, local or world leaders with whom we had the pleasure of being personally acquainted, Diamond never let us down. Like some charismatic spiritual leader, he provided us solace and inspiration with songs like "Holly Holy" and "Brother Love's Traveling Salvation Show," the closest that I ever came to being truly saved, with the possible exception of a subsequent teen tour in Israel. And while I personally never had an imaginary friend growing up, at least I had "Shilo," Diamond's great song about imagining a special pal.

In *What About Bob?*, a 1991 film comedy, the title character played by Bill Murray offered his intriguing world view that "there are two types of people in the world: those who like Neil Diamond and those who *don't*." In the movie, Bob emphatically did *not* like Diamond. Then again, Bob was an obsessive-compulsive psychiatric patient with major issues and questionable judgment.

We Wilds, on the other hand, were in the far wiser former group of lifelong, red-white-and-Jew Diamondheads. My older brother, Jeff, and younger sister, Wendy, had become Diamondheads almost by association. For his part, my father, Stanley, also greatly admired the work of Neil Diamond, though truth be told, he was, and always would be, much more of a Frank Sinatra man. There was no *Sopranos*-like crime in that, particularly in Frank's native Garden State where we all lived as opposed to those "Brooklyn Roads" that Diamond had traveled on his way to the top.

Especially after my father moved out of our home sometime in the mid-seventies, the exceedingly male yet deeply sensitive adult voice of our favorite "Solitary Man" became all the more welcome at 25 Glenwood Road, which was apparently not walking distance to that "Glory Road" about which Diamond so poetically sang. Our biggest family sing-along was the almost absurdly catchy and life-affirming "Song Sung Blue," or "Song Sung Jew" as we sometimes sang with a certain unsubtle but sweet Semitic charm.

All these years and one-way memories later, Neil Diamond—the man, the myth, the middle-aged Hebrew hunk—was speaking to us not through blown-out car speakers, but far more directly, person to person—or at least superstar to person. Actually, truth be told, Diamond was speaking first and foremost to my mother.

"Carol, it's an *honor* to meet you," Neil Diamond told her warmly. "Your son David tells me that you've been listening to my music for years. I want you to know I *so* appreciate it."

A few months earlier, I had interviewed Neil Diamond for a long and loving piece in *Rolling Stone* magazine, exactly the sort of supposedly hip magazine that had often dismissed this legendary singer-songwriter and performer, who has long been the people's choice as opposed to a critics' darling. The fact that Neil had generously donated to an antigun charity that publisher Jann Wenner had founded to honor his fallen friend John Lennon probably didn't hurt either.

Despite selling more than a hundred million records—or perhaps *because* of selling more than a hundred million records—Neil Diamond had gotten pretty much everything in this world except the respect as an artist that he rightly deserved. Everyone from Frank Sinatra to Bob Dylan sang his songs, and even the uberhip Miles Davis sang his praises. But for some it was never quite enough. For me, he was something much more worthwhile than hip; he was *good*. Make that *great*. And so, if showing Diamond that core respect right there in black and white meant that I would risk earning the scorn of some of my groovier-than-thou *Rolling Stone* colleagues, well, then so be it. After some soul searching, I ultimately decided that to deny my love for all things Diamond was to deny my very identity.

For his part, perhaps sensing my knowledge and affection for his work, Diamond was less guarded with me than he had been with interviewers in the past. I first asked him about his immortalized performance alongside the likes of Bob Dylan, Joni Mitchell, Neil Young, and Van Morrison at The Last Waltz, the 1976 farewell performance by the acclaimed rock group The Band on Thanksgiving Day, which was famously filmed by Martin Scorsese. Diamond was invited to take part in The Last Waltz because The Band's Robbie Robertson had produced Diamond's 1976 album, *Beautiful Noise*. He sang a beautiful version of one of his stellar songs from that album, called "Dry Your Eyes." Yet, I pointed out, despite the fact that he was likely far and away the single best-selling recording artist at the Winterland Ballroom in San Francisco that night, there was still a curious sense of his being somehow apart and different from the other rock icons in the room.

"I don't fit in," Diamond confessed to me. "But you could put me in *any* show and I wouldn't fit in. You could put me in a rock show and I wouldn't fit in. You could put me in a country show and I wouldn't fit in. You could put me onstage with Sinatra and I wouldn't fit in. . . . I just do *not* fit in. . . . I'm sorry. I apologize to everybody. But I never tried to fit in, because that meant conforming what I could write or what I could do to a certain set of rules. . . . The last group I remember joining was the Boy Scouts, and they threw me out for nonpayment of dues. So I suppose you could say that I've always gone my own way."

I had flown to Los Angeles from New York to meet my hero, expecting him to be some splashy star-spangled figure, like Elvis in Vegas. Yet the man I met turned out to be infinitely more approachable and down-to-earth than that. Unshaven and dressed in jeans and casual shirts, he struck me as a far cooler and more interesting presence than his naysayers would ever bother to imagine.

As Diamond told me years later, from his point of view he was no Elvis, Jewish or otherwise. "When I first came up it was Elvis that was king and I was much more clean cut," he confessed. "He was black leather jackets and motorcycles, and I was just a nice kid who minded his manners and helped his dad out in the store after school every day." Those who knew him in the beginning say Elvis too was actually a nice kid from Tupelo who loved his mama before he rocked the world.

As musical superstars who lived in Malibu went, Diamond was turning out to be a real *haymish* kind of famous guy from Brooklyn. For all he had been through, he was still at heart the New York boy who went to Erasmus High on Flatbush Avenue, where Bernard Malamud, Barbara Stanwyck, Mae West, and Mickey Spillane had gone before him—as had a young girl named Barbra Joan Streisand who sang with him in the school's hundred-member fixed chorus and who would later become a perfect duet partner. For the record, Diamond then graduated from Abraham Lincoln High on Ocean Parkway, which also gave the world Joseph Heller, Mel Brooks, Neil "The Other Neil" Sedaka, Carole King, and even Marv Albert.

Diamond was well aware that not everyone was a Diamondhead, but as he explained in *Rolling Stone*, that did not stop him for a moment from achieving his musical mission of touching me, touching you. "When you have done so many songs over the years, one of them has to have attracted at least somebody, you know? If you haven't liked one song that I've written, then I should probably hang it up. I tried for twenty years to get everybody to like at least one song. And if I haven't done that by now, I'll just have to spend the next twenty years trying to do it."

Having loved the guy's music forever, I found that I liked the actual man behind the music just as much. This was a lesson that I would learn again and again over the next twenty years: the bigger they were, the better they were to know. I would have the pleasure of spending time with three of the four Beatles, for instance, and found them all to be genuinely Fab. The Backstreet Boys, who would arrogantly keep me outside in the cold for hours waiting to interview them for a cover story—not so much.

During our many hours of conversation over two days at Diamond's homey office on a tiny Los Angeles side street named Melrose Place, I had apparently mentioned that I was in fact a second-generation Diamond worshipper. Immediately after my article ran in the magazine, Diamond had written a very warm thank-you note on his personal stationery, which bore an engraved illustration of a frog wearing a crown, a charmingly self-deprecating reference to a famous line from "I Am . . . I Said," perhaps Diamond's most self-revelatory classic about being "a frog who dreamed of bein' a king and then became one." A few weeks later, his trusty publicist, Sherrie Levy, called to say that Neil wanted to invite my family and me to attend his show in New Jersey as his guest. And that, I assumed, would be the end of my relationship with Mr. Neil Diamond.

Now here we stood just minutes before showtime in Diamond's large, welcoming dressing room. Spread all around us were assorted signed items of merchandise: Neil Diamond T-shirts, posters, tour books, and CDs. Neil explained to my mother that it was all for her, a small token of his esteem. "You raised a real *mensch*," he said with a broad smile, "and I want you to know I *really* appreciate it." Having already gotten all the press he was ever likely to get from *Rolling Stone*, Neil Diamond had done everything for my mother short of bringing her flowers.

Predictably, my mother beamed with pure maternal pride and perhaps with some less pure feeling toward Diamond as well. For my part, I was dumbstruck in a somewhat different manner. Though only four years out of college, I had already become a journalist of sorts, ever so slightly jaded about seeing stars up close and personal. Yet this grand gesture of generosity was stunning. After all of the not-so good times we'd been through together as a family, it was moving to see my mother so well treated by our very own family icon. There was, you might say—at least if you were an aging Jewish rock critic like me—a whole lot of *nachas* going on.

It took a moment to fully grasp the reality that I had just been dubbed a *mensch* in good standing by Neil Diamond himself. As I remember it, my mother was left speechless and found herself in a highly emotional state that the even vaguely Yiddish speaking among us will recognize as a full-body *kvell*. If so, one could hardly blame her since she had suddenly found herself in the presence of true pop royalty. Diamond looked every bit the part. Only moments before he was about to take the stage—and I mean, really take it—Diamond was already made up and dressed to kill onstage in all his now-familiar glitz and glory. Despite being the man who brought the world "Forever in Blue Jeans," Diamond had long had a far less casual way of dressing for his fans. At just under six feet, the man was both taller and skinnier than he photographed, and a *lot* taller and skinnier than anyone who had ever dipped their toes in the shallow genetic wading pool of the Wilds. For tonight's show, he was wearing black pants and one of those white, shiny-almost-metallic, open-necked stage peasant blouses that he stressed were made not of sequins, as commonly but wrongly theorized, but rather *beads*.

At one point I pulled myself together long enough to thank Diamond for this abundant and unexpected act of generosity. "Thank *you*, buddy," he said blessedly loud enough for the rest of my family to hear. For once, payback was not a bitch, but rather a *mensch*.

Just then a loud knock on Diamond's dressing room door served to remind us where we were and why we were there in the first place. As if he actually had any doubts, Diamond asked us to "try and enjoy the show." Then right before we were hurriedly escorted back to our seats before the lights dimmed and the show began, Diamond made one small request: "Carol," he asked gallantly. "Would you mind terribly taking a photo with me?" A photographer emerged from out of the shadows of the Brendan Byrne hallway, and somehow we all jumped into the shot and a quick photo was snapped, forever documenting a moment of actual shared joy just before we returned to our seats to hear our new buddy Neil's beautiful noise.

For two decades now, that very same photo has stood on my mother's bedside table. And even though the picture caught me in one of my least attractive phases (and that's marking on one hell of a steep curve) I still look upon that image fondly, even if I do appear to be retaining much of the Hudson River as I hide behind a temporary beard and a supersized overcoat.

Good times never seemed so good, and rarely would again.

I'M A BELIEVER

I'm a man of God
Though I never learned to pray
Walked the pathways of the heart
Found him there along the way

—"MAN OF GOD," BY NEIL DIAMOND

ALBERT EINSTEIN, WHO WAS APPARENTLY A PRETTY FAIR FIDDLER, once offered his informed view that "God does not play dice." Still, if He really does exist, I tend to believe that God *does* play guitar, likely quite well. In my mind at least, He plays rhythm parts mostly, but perhaps the occasional flashy lead too. And self-evidently being one of those dreaded "creative sorts," there is reason to believe that He may very well *write* songs too.

The first time I ever enjoyed the semireligious experience of speaking with Neil Diamond at his former office on Melrose Place, I could not help but notice that the man whom I had been closely listening to my entire life displayed a charming, if unorthodox and vaguely pagan, tendency to bestow upon those individuals whom he greatly admired the honorary title of "god." "He's a *god*," Diamond would say repeatedly during our conversation, or only slightly less frequently, "She's a *god*," suggesting that while this uplifting man who put "Brother Love's

Traveling Salvation Show" on the road may not be much of a monotheist, he is definitely not a sexist either.

By upgrading men and women to such heavenly status, Diamond was obviously seeking to fully express his profound respect for all the extraordinary songwriters of the Brill Building era, all of whom had managed to rise to the ranks of the big time years before he ever did. Over the years, Diamond has reflected frequently on that significant turning period in his life, including on one of his greatest albums ever, *Beautiful Noise* (1976), and on a later tribute album called *Up on the Roof: Songs from the Brill Building* (1993). When Neil speaks of that era, he tends to take great pains to stress that he himself was simply a very minor character in one of the greatest pop stories ever told and not one of those gifted musical deities whom he worshipped in his early days as a singer-songwriter in Tin Pan Alley.

The way Diamond tells it, he was merely some struggling low-level *schlep* trying to peddle his second-rate songwriting wares to little or no interest. The reigning gods of song, meanwhile, were the likes of Carole King and Gerry Goffin, Jerry Leiber and Mike Stoller, a younger and at least slightly more innocent Phil Spector, Doc Pomus and Mort Shuman, Barry Mann and Cynthia Weil, Neil Sedaka and Howie Greenfield, Burt Bacharach and Hal David, and, last but hardly least, Ellie Greenwich and Jeff Barry, who would eventually produce and collaborate on Diamond's classic early hits like "Cherry, Cherry" and "Solitary Man."

So before we get to fully telling His story, please allow me the chance to share my praise right up front. When it comes to Neil Diamond, he is, I say, very much a musical god. To me, he's long been a very American idol, and not a false one either. This works out quite well because I'm a Believer. Chances are excellent that if you have read even this far, you're at least a partial Believer too. As for all ye of little faith and less taste when it comes to all things Diamond, please read on anyway, for you are hereby forgiven. You know not what you've been missing.

Lest we forget, God is no stranger in the songs of Neil Diamond. Taking a quick scan through my own iPod, I soon found the following songs that I have filed under His name:

"Thank the Lord for the Night Time"
"Brother Love's Traveling Salvation Show"
"Lordy"
"Walk on Water"
"Dear Father"
"The Good Lord Loves You"
"Heaven Can Wait"
"Holly Holy"
"Jerusalem"
"Leave a Little Room for God"
"Man of God"

Diamond has also recorded very nice cover versions of the Jewish prayer of atonement, "Kol Nidre," and the Beach Boys' "God Only Knows"—and that's not even mentioning all the times that Neil freely throws the word "Lordy" into a song, as he does in "Stones," "Captain Sunshine," and "Crunchy Granola Suite," to name just a few. And to be entirely ecumenical about the whole thing, let's not forget about "You Make It Feel Like Christmas," one of Neil's heartwarming eighties compositions, whatever your faith happens to be. Then there is the stocking-stuffing set of traditional Yuletide classics on which Diamond puts his own Semitic spin, on his two popular Christmas albums.

For my *gelt*, *nobody* rocks "Jingle Bell Rock" like Neil.

Truth be told, there is something mysterious, if not holier than thou, about this man with a deep voice. He's not simply solitary, but also at least a little otherworldly. I remember that Elvis Costello, another one of my own musical gods growing up in the innocence of the Garden State, spoke of playing a show at Hollywood High early in his career and being taken aback, and even unnerved, when his famous record-label mate Neil Diamond stopped by on his tour bus. In particular, Costello remembered being struck by the sight of Diamond wearing a hat that read "Arch Angel," the chosen name of his personal recording studio.

"I thought that I was having some sort of religious vision," the British, non-Jewish Elvis told me, still shaking his head at the memory many years later. Somehow I got the sense that Costello, who quite likely may have been enjoying a little "Red, Red Wine" in those days, was not *entirely* sure at the time if Diamond's visitation was from some sort of musical devil or angel. Either way, Neil Diamond had made a powerful, unearthly impression on this new Elvis, as he has made on so many of us.

As for myself, I'm a Believer not just in the *existence* of Neil Diamond—because as far as I know no one yet has been foolish enough to be an outright Diamond denier—I'm a Believer in the enduring excellence of Diamond and the eternal healing power of His music in our lives. Consider this book to be simply one sinner's sincere effort to speak to the faithful and spread his good word about His great music to all those who need it—and can pay full retail.

Say "Amen," somebody! Then if the spirit moves you, say "*Mazel tov*" too.

I'm a Believer and have been one since at least the age of thirteen, when I was officially scheduled to become a man. At least that's when the Wild family bravely broke ground for the tacky, shallow-minded bar mitzvah that would be followed by having a rock-and-roll theme at my kids' table. Posters of my musical favorites—the Beatles, the Rolling Stones, the Eagles, Crosby, Stills, Nash and Young, Cat Stevens, and, the only Jew in the pack, Neil Diamond—all hung high above the kids as they consumed their Tamcrest Country Club salads with French dressing and the roast beef *au jus*. In the pictures that survive of that historic event, the scene looks not unlike the Last Supper, only with a few more Jews. In the 2006 film *Keeping Up with the Steins* starring Jeremy "Let's Hug It Out, Bitch" Piven, Neil Diamond agrees to actually play a bar mitzvah. We should only have been so lucky.

I'm a Believer that Bill Murray's title character in *What About Bob?* was totally correct. There really *are* two kinds of people: those who like Neil Diamond and those who don't. That being said, I am convinced after much soul searching that at least half the people who claim they don't like Neil Diamond actually, secretly, privately *do*. If you were to, say, hide in the backseat of one of these people's cars before a long drive—and at the behest of Da Capo's legal department, I am *not* suggesting you actually try this at home—I believe you would more likely than not hear this purported, theoretical nonfan singing along joyfully to whatever Neil Diamond song might happen to come on the radio, *especially* if it's "Sweet Caroline" or "Cracklin' Rose." Furthermore, I believe that somewhere, carefully hidden away in their imaginary CD or record collection, you would find at least one of the dozens of Neil Diamond's greatest hits collections. Even more shockingly, in their stacks of DVDs or a dusty VHS collection, in an accessible closet, attic, or basement, you might very well find a covered-up, supersecret copy of *The Jazz Singer* or even, may God help them, *Jonathan Livingston Seagull*.

The other fifty percent of those seriously misguided individuals who claim to be Neil naysayers are probably being one hundred percent honest when they make the shocking and outrageous claim to "not be fans." They are, nonetheless, also one hundred percent wrong. While casting no aspersions whatsoever about their moral character, they are probably either utterly pretentious poseurs or totally vicious bastards. I make these charges with all due respect. To each their own, after all.

Yet in my heart of hearts—my "Heartlight," if you will—I remain a firm Believer that if you hate Neil Diamond, then you may actually hate yourself.

I'm a Believer that Neil Diamond is an altogether merciful and loving musical god who looks kindly upon all those who follow his path. Once I asked Neil to define his average fan, and he immediately noted with a warm smile, "They're all *well* above average." In 2001, I questioned him again to discuss his dedicated following for his scandal-challenged but still interesting *Behind the Music* episode for which I served as producer. "They're people who follow their own guts," Neil said of his fans. "And it just so happens that over the years enough of them have gathered together to really create a large constituency for my music. And thank God for them."

Thank God, indeed.

At the same time, Diamond also acknowledged that, like him, his beloved, dedicated following was never considered especially hip either. While discussing his gifted contemporaries from way over in Queens—Simon and Garfunkel—Diamond noted that "their audience was much more intellectual, liberal, you know? Hipper. But then everybody's audience was hipper than mine . . . What can I say? I was left with the rest of America."

I'm a Believer that the mostly chaste love between Neil Diamond and his fans is something special: something deep and soulful and true. This close connection is based partly on shared experience and entirely on shared humanity. In the introduction to his excellent book *Always Magic in the Air: The Bomp and Brilliance of the Brill Building Era*, Ken Emerson quotes from Michael Chabon's novel *The Amazing Adventures of Kavalier and Clay*, in which one of the characters is said to have "dreamed the usual Brooklyn dreams of flight and transformation and escape."

Those same grand themes—of flight, transformation, and escape, as well as the eternal theme of the search for love—have haunted and graced Diamond's work from the very beginning. Somehow he has managed to transform those profoundly personal issues into one of the most successful acts of group therapy in musical history. Neil Diamond sings songs about isolation in a way that inevitably, and even magically, brings people together. This is the central paradox of the entire seventies singer-songwriter movement for which Diamond helped pave the way. At its core, it's all about alienation as a curiously comforting group activity. And thanks to that almost comically deep and perfectly imperfect voice of his, Diamond has artfully explored those issues always like a man and not just a "Two Bit Manchild." He reached out for decades and connected with millions of us as both a poet and a pop star.

I'm a Believer that Neil Diamond has thus more than earned a rightful place in the Rock and Roll Hall of Fame, an organization that has repeatedly and wrongly overlooked the cultural contributions of one of the most popular recording and performing artists of the twentieth and now twenty-first centuries. For years, I've been asked to vote once the nominees are selected, and I never recall having seen Neil's name on the short list. Suffice to say, considering the fact that Miles Davis and Madonna are already in the Rock and Roll Hall of Fame, I hereby pledge *never* to return to Cleveland until Neil

Diamond is there too. Of course, I wasn't exactly planning a trip to Cleveland anyway, but I hope that the sentiment comes across all the same.

When I first interviewed Neil for *Rolling Stone*, the headline was a memorable question that Diamond himself posed to me at one point in the conversation: "Am I a rock person, or what the hell am I?" Because Neil has enjoyed tremendous success with numerous romantic ballads over the years, there are those who have exiled him from the rock section of record stores. Based on my own informal survey of the situation, even in those relatively few music stores still left in this doomy digital era, Neil Diamond continues to be the victim of a curious kind of record store apartheid, too often cast aside to a distant, secondary store section often dubbed "Vocals," "Pop," "Middle of the Road," or the dreaded "Easy Listening," the rock-and-roll retail equivalent of a premature burial.

Yet make no mistake, as far as I know, there has never been a Neil Diamond show where the man did *not* rock, with the possible exception of that time in November 1985 when Neil went to dinner at the White House during the administration of Ronald Reagan. That night, Nancy Reagan stood before the guests and asked if Diamond would consider singing for the Reagans' honored guests, Prince Charles and Princess Diana. Neil politely agreed and sang two of his big ballads—"September Morn" and "You Don't Bring Me Flowers"— for all the invited dignitaries. So okay, that gig possibly did *not* rock, being both ballad-heavy and in a Republican White House. Then again, let us not forget that immediately after his performance, Princess Diana personally asked Neil to dance. In a royal, respectful and yet still sexy way, that probably *did* rock.

During that first conversation, Diamond quite rightly answered his own question about whether he was in fact a "rock person" and, significantly, he did so in the affirmative. "Well, the answer is yes, my music is based on rock music," Neil explained. "But I also have a tremendous love for the romantic music that came before rock, partially because it's in my tradition. But all of my music is based on rock, you know. If Roy Orbison is rock, if the Everly Brothers are rock, if Elvis Presley is rock, if the Beatles are rock, then yes, I am."

See, He is . . . He said.

As I see it, the truth is that Neil rocks whenever he wants to. "I'm like the Will Rogers of pop," Diamond once told the *Los Angeles Times*. "There isn't a musical form I've heard that I haven't liked."

When I interviewed him for *Behind the Music*, Paul Shaffer, who had long led the band at the Rock and Roll Hall of Fame induction ceremony as well as on David Letterman's shows, made it clear that in his highly educated view, the pending matter of Neil Diamond being part of rock and roll was to be considered settled law. "How can you deny that Neil Diamond is a seminal rock artist and writer?" he asked. "You *can't* deny it."

Should that expert testimony not be good enough for you, take it from the very man who starred in *School of Rock*, Jack Black, with whom Neil would appear in the 2001 Diamond-centric film comedy, *Saving Silverman*. When I spoke with the actor and coleader of the most rocking band in the land, Tenacious D, for that same *Behind the Music* show, he freely said the following of Diamond: "He's a showman. He's from the *showman* school of rock and roll."

That very telling comment by Jack Black may reveal part of Neil Diamond's mysterious crime in the opinion of some of his more doubting critics. Year after year, the man has been caught in the act of going well out of his way to actually *entertain* the people who show up to see him. Remarkably, in our age of irony and celebrated idiocy, this sort of ongoing commitment to pleasing audiences may be, for some,

Neil Diamond's original sin, showmanship being somehow less hip than self-indulgent angst or navel-gazing.

I'm a Believer that the appeal of Neil is, nonetheless, universal. As far as I know, I have not traveled to other planets. Yet once during the early days of the First Gulf War, following a trip to London and Amsterdam with a great band called Prefab Sprout, I did find myself on vacation in a open-air market in Agadir, Morocco, looking around to see what English-speaking artists had recordings available there for purchase. I had always dreamed of trying to haggle in an Arab nation, plus the market was next to a particularly tasty couscous joint.

There among the bootlegs, in assorted languages that I could not read, I remember seeing only three albums that I recognized: Michael Jackson's *Bad*, Led Zeppelin's *Houses of the Holy*, and Neil Diamond's *The Jazz Singer*. Sure, they were all bootleg copies, and it appeared highly unlikely that any royalties would be forthcoming. Still, seeing a guy from Brooklyn striking a dramatic pose on the cover of such a defiantly American album was a welcome if slightly bizarre sight in that Moroccan bazaar.

See, I'm a Believer that Neil Diamond didn't just go on *American Idol* this year—he *is* an American idol, year after year. That's because I'm a Believer that Neil Diamond didn't just write a great and beautiful song called "America." I believe that Neil Diamond is part of a great and beautiful song called America and, trust me, this downright patriotic sentiment is coming from a normally wiseass Democrat.

I'm a Believer that the very fact that Neil Diamond attended New York University on a fencing scholarship says so much about him and his unique version of the American Dream. In my entire family history, the only known fencing Jew was a relative who was said to fence stolen goods during the Great Depression. Like the old Yiddish proverb puts it, the Jew who can gracefully fence is a Jew who can record two popular Christmas albums without ever tacking on even one Chanukah chestnut.

Okay, so maybe that's a *new* Yiddish proverb.

Either way, I've written this book not to get something out of my system, so much as to take a long and largely loving look at how and why Neil Diamond's music became part of my system, and I presume, part of yours as well.

As much as I'm a Believer—and proud to shout that out loudly in these pages—I hereby confess that I too have entertained a few stray shards of Diamond doubts over the years. As gods go, Neil Diamond is not one of your most omniscient overlords. And as much as I am moved by the way that he sings the song "Walk on Water," I understand full well that the man himself walks on earth, generally one foot in front of the other much like the rest of us. This harsh reality dawned on me during our first interview, when we got into our first and only real disagreement regarding a matter of no small significance to me, namely, the precise number of songs he had written that the Monkees ever recorded.

We, of course, agreed on all the obvious tracks: "I'm a Believer," the classic #1 hit for the Monkees that Diamond originally wrote with country superstar Eddy Arnold in mind rather than the Monkees, "Look Out (Here Comes Tomorrow)," and "Little Bit Me, Little Bit You," which eventually hit #2 for the Pre-Fab Four. It's easy to forget that once upon a poppier time, having these compositions of his recorded by the arguably more primitive Monkees played a significant part in Diamond's evolution as a widely recognized singer-songwriter.

The flashpoint for our first fight came over a fourth Diamond composition called "Love to Love," recorded by the Monkees in the same era though unreleased until much later. This long-lost gem sounds like a variation of "I'm a Believer" with Davy Jones on lead vocals backed by a band that sounds more like the Byrds than the Monkees. For his part, Diamond claimed to have absolutely no memory whatsoever of this recording. Brothers and sisters, I ask you, what sort of musical god is it that could deny his very own creation? With a heavy heart—and inevitably at least a few other heavy body parts as well—I am here to confess to you that at least until I sent him a recorded copy of this long-lost Monkees rarity, Diamond did *exactly* that. To his credit, he then apologized profusely for his very human mistake. This was the exact moment of truth when I realized that perhaps I had come to know some aspects of Diamond's life better than he did, although in Diamond's defense, he had no doubt been busy actually *living* that life.

Imagine, then, my terrible shame when in researching this book I discovered yet another pop rock Rosetta Stone that I had left unturned. It turns out that on January 27, 1967, the Monkees recorded, yet never released, a fifth Diamond song called "Black & Blue (from Kickin' Myself)." The fact that this crucial bit of Neil-centric information had escaped my attention powerfully suggests that I am *not* a god, which surprised my wife not even for a moment.

Let the record reflect that Neil Diamond has never claimed to be perfect. And even to my loving ears and eyes, there have been a few songs and maybe more than a couple of outfits that clearly suggest a certain appealingly human fallibility. He has, however, achieved omnipresence through his songs. Like the song says, everybody knows one.

There are songs with which I have my own long-term love-hate relationship, such as the *E.T.*-inspired "Heartlight." I understand how people could find the song, inspired as it was by seeing *E.T.*, to be a little heavy-handed and emotionally manipulative. On the other hand, none of that means that I have not wept openly listening to the song from time to time. Furthermore, as someone with mostly mixed feelings about the look and sound of the eighties in general, Neil's eighties hit "Headed to the Future"—his most recent pop hit to date—sounds to these ears to be the single most dated thing he ever recorded.

Beyond those two tunes, there is at least one song that decades after its initial release still scares me, namely, "The Pot Smoker's Song" from Diamond's memorably titled 1968 album *Velvet Gloves and Spit*. This musical example of genuine reefer madness is an early antidrug song that curiously blended upbeat pop with audio vérité monologues from real-life addicts at the Phoenix House in New York. For obvious reasons, this was not a song that helped Diamond's standing in the hip community, insomuch as there *is* a hip community. When we spoke of this rare lapse in musical judgment for *Rolling Stone*, Diamond told me, "Part of me is rebellious. And part of me will do something like that just to say, 'Hey, fuck you.' That's all it is. Fortunately, that side of me doesn't come out too often."

Diamond went on to say that in retrospect he had probably misnamed the song, since most of the people he had met at the Phoenix House were heroin addicts, not potheads: "So to the hip community, you know, it was more evidence that Neil Diamond was not one of their kind of guys. It was genuine; it was heartfelt. But it also confirmed a lot of people's feelings that I wasn't hip."

Personally, I consider Neil Diamond to be one of the hippest individuals I have ever met, and I *still* don't like "The Pot Smoker's Song" even one toke, even though I've never personally inhaled . . . at least not that I can clearly remember.

Here's another true confession: for all my many years of admiration, to the very day I write these words, I have never even dared to actually watch the film version of *Jonathan Livingston Seagull*. Though I've come to quite like much of Diamond's ambitious music from the movie, I always figured you had to be *really* high to watch such a bird-brained movie. For this book, I will seek to finally rectify that personal lapse of mine. Wish me luck.

I'm a Believer that Neil Diamond's long life in music is proof positive that frequently it is the masses who all too often understand things long before the critics catch on. As Neil once told me matter-of-factly, "I had to make a decision early in my career: Am I to please the critics? Or am I to please the audience? And I thought it was more democratic to try and please the audience."

Democracy has rarely sounded so good.

Let me share with you here two dirty little secrets about rock critics. The first is that until what President Bush so wisely called "the Internets" came along and made our media world a far more open place, critics were too rarely held accountable for what they wrote, outside of the stray outraged Letter to the Editor. In my own case, I can only think of two exceptions where my egomaniacal ramblings were really called into question.

The first came when I made the entirely foolhardy decision to publicly pan the Grateful Dead's *Shakedown Street* album in my first weeks as a student-journalist at Loomis Chaffee, a small Connecticut prep school where even one of the teachers played in a Dead cover band. Ultimately, I was fortunate enough to survive this dopey public act of aggressively anti-tie dye treachery, but only after a long weekend of placing myself on a critic relocation program for my own safety. The second time was when I heard, albeit indirectly, that *Miami Vice* sensation Don Johnson wanted to kick my fat ass for describing him in a review of his 1986 album *Heartbeat* as the Bobby Goldsboro of his generation. Apparently, this sockless superstar didn't realize that I meant this as a compliment. The other dirty little secret of critics is that, much like the human beings whom they only partially resemble, these otherwise contrary creatures actually want to be wanted, and need to be needed. As a result, these critical sorts are particularly tough on major pop phenomena that they play absolutely no part in creating. As with any group given to the danger of groupthink, critics tend to discount pop phenomena that were anointed not by their mighty pens but by the far mightier power of paying customers. Critics also tend to find ways to overlook the obvious. I think back to what Neil's costar in *The Jazz Singer* said when she was asked to analyze Diamond's appeal for *Behind the Music*. "I mean, he writes really great music," Lucie Arnaz replied matter-of-factly. "He's also really cute. Women faint. He's got great hair."

Putting the matter of hair aside, I don't think it helped matters much that a largely New York–based media world—which, let's face facts, really does include no shortage of Jews—sometimes viewed Diamond as someone who early on in his career flew the coop from those "Brooklyn Roads" to sunny El Lay, that city of questionable angels. In this reductive view, Neil Diamond was sometimes wrongly portrayed as a sort of well-tanned sell-out—another flighty West Coast transplant like Tony Robbins' character in *Annie Hall*—by folks who were far more likely to relate to Woody Allen's *nebbishy* Alvy Singer. For too long, until his recent critical rediscovery in the light of his work with Rick Rubin on his last two albums, this most famous fencing Jew found himself in a sort of contest that one rarely wins—the kind waged with the media.

In the wake of my respectful *Rolling Stone* piece on Neil Diamond, I would have the pleasure of meeting and interviewing a number of other misunderstood and undervalued pop superstars, some who even sought me out as being at least open-minded or possibly a total pushover in the working pop culture press. Over the years that followed, I would get to hang often with Julio . . . Iglesias. I would bond beautifully with Barry . . . Manilow. I'd even wing around the world for a time with Paul and the lovely Linda . . . yes, McCartney.

In each case, I would discover that simply giving a fair hearing is often the perfect gift for the superstar who has absolutely *everything* except the sort of critical appreciation that rarely seems to arrive in print. Having this sort of experience taught me a critical lesson about human nature. Give someone creative the world and, more often than not, they will search that world for the one thing they *cannot* have and cannot get enough of. Often that's fair recognition for their best work.

I'll never forget one long day and night spent working on a cover story about Billy Joel, another notable American singer-songwriter and performer who continues to please millions, decades after some rock scribes wrote him off. Early in one of our days together, while Joel and his band were rehearsing at a Long Island police armory for an arena tour, the Piano Man insisted to me that he didn't "give a damn" about what the critics said to him. Later that very same night, after a few beers and more sambucas than I could count, the very same Innocent Man sat in the bar of my Holiday Inn on the Island quoting chapter and verse of ancient bad reviews, word for word, from memory. The fact that Joel's songs were timeless had somehow not lessened the hurt of otherwise forgotten words from old newspapers that had long ago yellowed and blown away with the wind.

In Neil Diamond's song "Done Too Soon," which sounds like it may have heavily influenced Billy Joel's later smash "We Didn't Start the Fire," he lists a series of famous historical figures, starting off with Jesus Christ and Fanny Brice. I believe it was Brice and not Jesus who once said, "Your audience gives you everything you need. They tell you." Diamond seems to have learned this lesson, taking his cues from his followers and not a smaller group of detractors.

As a recovering rock critic today, I'm a Believer that at heart Neil Diamond is first and foremost a songwriter. Neil himself would agree— at least he did going back to a 1976 interview with Noel Coppage in *Family Weekly.* "Songwriting is what I do," Diamond said then. "Performing is the easiest part of what I do, and songwriting is the hardest. Songs are so all encompassing; they're the joys and sorrows and pacing of life. Songwriting is the only real discipline I've had in my whole life—that's why I hate it so much; I don't *like* imposing that kind of discipline on myself, but it has to be. Songs are life in 80 words or less."

I'm a Believer that Neil Diamond is ultimately *sui generis,* truly one of a kind. "There is nobody else who *sounds* like him," Ellie Greenwich said of her former protégé. "There is nobody else that *writes* like him."

Despite that, the Neil Diamond whom I have come to know offstage is more given to self-deprecation than any sort of bravado. In early times, there were interviews that suggested this was a man of great confidence, with even a dash of cockiness. One remark that some made much of came during a 1971 interview with a then-cool, now-defunct rock magazine called *Crawdaddy.* "I don't think I'll be a phenomenon until I'm dead," Diamond was quoted as saying, "because then someone will turn around and say, 'Jesus Christ, look at what that man wrote.' I figure it'll take about twenty years of writing, because I'm going to spread so much good music around this world, you're not going to believe it."

Thirty-five years after he shared those words, what strikes me is not so much a certain notable nerviness or hint of arrogance, but rather an almost stunning foresight: a single-minded vision that one man has already made true against considerable odds. Think of how many kids with a guitar dared to dream of having that kind of impact. Then think of how many actually made it all come true.

And when it comes to Neil Diamond, the measure of the artist, if not the measure of the man, is all right there in his songs. Until his book comes along, the songs together represent quite a telling autobiography. As Diamond once told me, "I think if people listen to my songs they know my story and they know who I am." And to quote a song written by a fallen Brill Building god named Phil Spector, to know him is to love him.

I proudly profess to love much of Diamond's catalog, and at minimum, he has written at least two of my top-ten favorite songs of all time. The first is "Play Me," an endlessly romantic song that Bono and his brethren in U2 saw fit to perform part of on tour a few years back. This is not simply one of Diamond's loveliest songs, it is also exceedingly revealing in the way it suggests just how closely connected Diamond is with his music. The song's simple yet stunning chorus is proof that at his best Diamond is a genuine romantic poet:

> *You are the sun*
> *I am the moon*
> *You are the words*
> *I am the tune*
> *Play me*

When I asked him about the song, he said that originally he couldn't decide what would be the proper time signature for "Play Me." He recalled how Richard Bennett, who played guitar on the session and worked with Diamond for many years, tried a guitar figure in three-quarter time and suddenly it was crystal clear that was how "Play

Me" should be heard. "So it ended up a waltz, and I guess that's what the song was meant to be," Neil explained.

My other all-time Neil Diamond favorite is another song that's absolutely everything it's meant to be: the slightly lesser known but entirely exquisite "And the Grass Won't Pay No Mind." Released as the flip side of Neil's African-tinged single "Soolaimon," this song was also recorded by Mark Lindsay of Paul Revere and the Raiders fame, and in a royally soulful rendition by Elvis Presley, who was briefly Neil's neighbor in Holmby Hills in the seventies.

Impressively, in just the past few years, Neil has written a number of brand new songs that for me rank right up with those past classics. For my tastes, there's "Oh Mary," the stunning opening track on his 2005 album, *12 Songs*, a song that seemed to announce a whole new golden era in Diamond's music. Then there's the wonderfully titled "Pretty Amazing Grace" on his latest album, 2008's *Home Before Dawn*. To be fair, it might take a decade or so for me to figure out exactly where these songs stand in Neil's pop pantheon, alongside more time-tested Diamond gems like "Solitary Man," "Shilo," "Brooklyn Roads," "Glory Road," "Sweet Caroline," "Cracklin' Rose," "If You Know What I Mean," "Can Anybody Hear Me?" and "I Haven't Played This Song in Years," among so many others.

I'm a Believer that much like both the Old Testament and New Testament—two of my all-time top-ten Testaments, if you were wondering—Neil Diamond's songs are open to interpretation and yet meaningful even when we can't fully understand their depths. In my tackier moods, I'm a Believer that another one of Neil Diamond's outstanding songs, "Longfellow Serenade," may in fact be one of the world's most elegant and tuneful dick jokes ever told. Even if my lowbrow hunch here is wrong, and this throbbing number *isn't* about some less poetic, more flesh-and-blood sort of longfellow, "Let me make it warm for you" and "Come on baby, ride" both sure sound like lusty come-ons.

I'm a Believer that Neil Diamond is one of the only songwriters in the world who could make international headlines by revealing the inspiration for a song that he wrote some four decades earlier. That's precisely what Diamond did when he finally let it be known in the winter of 2007 that "Sweet Caroline" was inspired by seeing a cute picture of young Caroline Kennedy in a magazine. "It was a picture of a little girl dressed to the nines in her riding gear, next to her pony," Diamond told the Associated Press. "It was such an innocent, wonderful picture, I immediately felt there was a song in there." This is possibly one reason that Diamond keeps finding great songs out in the ether: because then as now, he's always out there searching for them.

I'm a Believer that Neil Diamond deserves credit for bringing African sounds and instruments to a mainstream audience with his ambitious and accomplished 1970 album, *Tap Root Manuscript*. It featured his "African Trilogy," which included the left-field top-forty hit "Soolaimon" and brought some Third World soul to the rest of the world, more than a decade and a half before Paul Simon's masterful *Graceland*.

I'm a Believer that Neil Diamond's best songs are forever, and that man himself is looking pretty damn good for sixty-six too. Further, Diamond stands today as a shining example of daring to stick around as opposed to rock's preferred approach of self-destructing and dying young. At the ages of sixty-four and sixty-seven, when some contemporaries are packing it in creatively, Neil Diamond has now released two of the best albums of his entire life, *12 Songs* and *Home Before Dawn*. Sure, I loved Kurt Cobain as much as the next grungy guy, but frankly I'd far rather live long and prosper like Neil Diamond, who's managed to make millions of people of all ages happy long after he stopped smelling anything like Teen Spirit.

I'm a Believer that Neil Diamond is still the best of all possible Neil Diamonds. Specifically, he's even better than any of the many Diamond tribute acts on the market, such as Super Diamond with Surreal Neil; Fantastic Diamond; Jay White, who's America's Diamond Live; Cherry Cherry; Double Diamond; The Diamond Geezer; The Diamond Collection; Diamond Nights; Black Diamond; Nearly Neil and the Solitary Band; The Ultimate Diamond with Jack Berrios; Hot August Night; Rob Garrett, King of Diamonds; Marc Dobson's "So Good" Tribute; Tom Sadge; or even Diamond Is Forever with David Sherry.

On December 16, 2000—my birthday, for the love of God—my wife, Fran, and I were kindly invited to sit with Neil and his lovely Australian girlfriend, Rachel "Rae" Farley, at the House of Blues in West Hollywood, where he would witness the splendid spectacle of Super Diamond for the first time. Toward the end of Super Diamond's highly entertaining set, Neil leaned over to let me know that in a matter of mere minutes he would actually be taking the stage to sing with his own tribute act. Tragically, my otherwise goodhearted wife insisted that we had to leave the show before that since we had promised our babysitter we would be home by 11:00 p.m. And so, to her eternal shame and my eternal outrage, we actually left what would have been a religious experience as well as the single best birthday present this aging Jew could even imagine. With prayer and time, our marriage ultimately survived this almost certain recipe for "Love on the Rocks."

I'm a Believer that in any fair Neil-to-Neil test, Neil must be considered the single greatest Neil of all time, easily taking the title from the likes of former schoolmate and pop star Neil Sedaka, British Labour leader Neil Kinnock, Pet Shop Boy Neil Tennent, authors Neil

Postman and Neil Gaiman, Neil Peart of the progressive Canadian band Rush, and another true living legend who came to us from the Great White North, Neil Young. For the record, I find Neil Young to be as endlessly cool and raggedly glorious as the next aging, scruffy rock critic, but when push comes to shove among comparative Neils, I'm just going to have to buy American. Last but not least, when you think about it, even Neil Armstrong, the first man to walk on the moon, really only had that *one* big hit, while the more earthbound Diamond has already had close to forty.

I'm a Believer that for all the lite substitutes, *nobody* sings Diamond like Diamond. This reminds me of one of Neil's better light comedy moments in *The Jazz Singer,* when Lucie Arnaz's character tells Diamond's singer-songwriter character, "Nobody should sing your songs but you, Jess." No doubt drawing on his own days of struggle, Diamond answers, "So far, nobody has."

I'm a Believer that Neil Diamond may not in fact be the greatest actor in the world, but in *The Jazz Singer*, I remain convinced that he was better and more subtle than one of the greatest actors of all time, Sir Laurence Olivier. So by the theory of relativity, perhaps Neil Diamond *is* the greatest actor in the world, after all.

I'm a Believer that Neil Diamond deserves more Grammys than he has, and quite possibly a Noble Peace Prize for playing a cantor's son in *The Jazz Singer* and yet recording two Christmas albums.

I'm a Believer that Neil Diamond should be honored, damn it, not mocked, for dressing for success. I'm certain that Neil puts on those beaded shirts and sings his heart out not just for himself but for *us*. He understands full well that the faithful don't just want to see him—they *need* to see him in all his glory. In his free time, he's as much a scruffy man as a solitary man. Yet this slightly self-conscious kid from Brooklyn transforms himself because he knows that his fans look to him not just as a songwriter but as an indomitable showman as well. In 1996, Neil explained to Rachel Cook of London's the *Observer* that he really does become someone else entirely when he takes the stage. "I do everything but step in a phone booth to change," Diamond told her. "You put the costume on and it's part of becoming the other person. I have to have the uniform, or I can't fly." Performing, he said, "makes me feel less shy. Sometimes, I find such joy in it that it takes me to another place . . . not permanently, but for the two hours that I'm on stage, it takes me out of myself."

I'm a Believer that Neil Diamond is a truly tough act to follow, though after an early show with the Who at which Pete Townshend smashed his guitar, Diamond said, "*They* can follow me." For the record, Neil Diamond is also apparently a tough act to go on before as well. If you don't believe me, listen to the brilliant Albert Brooks (who was actually born Albert Einstein) discussing the difficulty of opening for an act as popular as Neil Diamond for a few years ("Memoirs of an Opening Act, Part 1" on his 1973 album *Comedy Plus One*). Beyond the occasional fan interrupting his comedy to cry out for "Kentucky Woman," Brooks seemed mostly taken with Diamond's growing popularity. "I started with him when he was doing small colleges and my god, I watched the man price himself right out of the business," he joked. "No, it was getting strange there towards the end. He would perform and the owner of the building would come and give him the deed to the building."

I'm a Believer that the relationship between Neil Diamond and his fans is a close and intimate one, at least as close and intimate as relationships get when largely confined to arenas, stadiums, and the occasional open-air amphitheater. It's good for Neil too, at least based on what songwriting god Ellie Greenwich says Neil once told her: "When you walk out on the stage, it is the *ultimate* orgasm."

I'm a Believer that the "Songs of Life" (to name a song from *The Jazz Singer*) Neil Diamond has given us for the last forty years accurately reflect the man. The impression one gets of Neil Diamond through his compositions is, in my limited but long-term experience, altogether both flattering and accurate. And so it is only because Neil Diamond has earned such a humanistic, good-natured persona over the years that comic genius Will Ferrell could do his memorable parody of Neil as a profoundly creepy, murderous, addicted, and racist sociopath. Ferrell's Diamond is oddly given to absentmindedly revealing his dark side in tortured stage patter, like explaining on a very special, imaginary episode of VH1's *Storytellers* that "America" was "fueled creatively by my massive hatred of immigrants," that "Forever in Blue Jeans" was written "after I killed a drifter to get an erection," and that "Cracklin' Rosie" was inspired by a passion for "hardcore barely legal porn." In this case of comedy, it's funny because it's *not* true. Also, I'm a Believer that Neil Diamond undeniably has a fully functioning sense of humor, as evidenced by the fact that in May of 2002 he actually agreed to appear alongside Ferrell on the comedian's last show as an *SNL* player.

I'm a Believer that consistency can be a virtue, and by almost any standard Neil Diamond possesses it. Consider the fact that Neil Diamond has had most of the same band members for more than thirty years. In a business with precious little loyalty, Diamond has been fiercely dedicated to his band, and they to him. Okay, sure, Diamond has been married and divorced twice, but let he who is without marital sin (especially in his generation) cast the first stone. Furthermore, Diamond has always been gallant, being the first to explain that he is not easy to live with and that those around him have had to pay a price for his lifelong dedication to his music.

In 1996, after twenty-five years together, Neil paid a reported $150 million in his divorce to his second wife, Marcia Murphey.

Rather than complain, Diamond was quoted at the time as saying of his ex-wife, "She's been through thick and thin with me and deserves half of my fortune." As I well know as the child of divorce, any marital split can be a profoundly painful experience for all involved. On the other hand, when you can write a check for $150 million—and that check clears—perhaps the message is that in addition to perhaps doing something wrong, you've also paradoxically been doing something *right*.

I'm a Believer because, both as a parent and a son, I have come to fully appreciate that, as a rule, the music of Neil Diamond does not scare older people or small children, or anyone in between. Whenever we sit together to talk about life for a few hours while our wives are out shopping, my father-in-law, Art Turk (who grew up just down those Brooklyn roads from the Diamond dry goods store), and I always put on some Neil Diamond music in the background. For us, and for many others of multiple generations, the music of Neil Diamond represents the very best and most solid kind of common ground.

Finally, I'm a Believer because of a very personal revelation that was offered unto me on the very day our firstborn son, Andrew, came into our lives (by coincidence in a hospital room about a minute from Neil Diamond's current office). As long as I live, I will never forget holding my son Andrew for the first time and realizing on some primal level that if I was going to communicate with this fetching young fellow, I would probably be better off singing to him than talking. First, I tried a little of Bob Dylan's "Blowin' in the Wind." He cried immediately, possibly because I do a fairly accurate Dylan imitation. Next up I tried the Beatles' "Yellow Submarine," which I sang with what I felt was a certain charming, Ringo-like gusto, if I do say so myself. Nonetheless, the review from my new son was similarly instant and equally negative.

Breaking into a parental sweat for the first but hardly the last time, I then dug deep into my own more pleasant childhood memories and decided it was time to break out something fail-safe. Lo and behold, the very second that I started crooning my most calming if ever so slightly off-key rendition of "Song Sung Blue," my little boy started cooing like—*exactly* like—a baby before dozing back to sleep.

Thank God for Neil Diamond. And to paraphrase a great song from the great man himself, thank the Lord for the nap time.

Song Sung 2

BROOKLYN ROADS, AND A FEW OTHER SIDE STREETS

Does some other young boy
Come home to my room?
Does he dream what I did, as he stands
By my window and looks out
On those Brooklyn Roads?

−"BROOKLYN ROADS," BY NEIL DIAMOND

GROWING UP IN NEW JERSEY, EVEN IN A PRIVILEGED COMMUNITY like Tenafly where my family lived, you come to realize that you're really ever only one exit away from a punch line—usually one at your expense. Eventually, you get used to it, sort of. Still, that doesn't mean that the occasional punch to the face can't hurt.

Today I understand full well that New Jersey jokes are a valid comedic genre unto themselves, few of them ever quite as elegant as Woody Allen's memorable line in "A Guide to Some of the Lesser Ballets" from his book *Without Feathers*: "The curtain rises on a vast primitive wasteland, not unlike certain parts of New Jersey."

That said, I never fully understood just how much a wasteland the Garden State was in the hearts and minds of the outside world, until one red hot but frustrating summer when I found myself spending a few fun and faith-filled weeks on a teen tour of Israel. My lifelong buddy Joey Bernstein and I were part of a blended group of young, horny, spoiled Jewish boys and girls from New Jersey, Long Island, Brooklyn and—to our considerable cultural shock—Birmingham, Alabama. Before long, Joey and I would discover the closely guarded secret among our people: there is nothing in the whole wide world quite as erotic as a woman with a Southern accent saying, *"Sh'ma Yisrael."* In our corner of the universe—as opposed to, say, Paris Hilton's—*that's* hot.

While making our way safely through the splendor of the Sinai Desert one hot afternoon, our posse of stray American princes and princesses and our armed guard stopped ever so briefly at what passed locally for a sort of extremely minimalist and sandy desert rest stop. If memory serves correctly, the proprietor of this humble establishment was a ragged-looking Bedouin gentleman in his thirties who, when we arrived, was baking some sort of thin, breadlike substance over what appeared to be aged camel-dung briquettes. Apparently, this was part of this fine fellow's questionable business plan—serving unappetizing refreshments to a bunch of Jewish kids living out some sweaty, Zionist version of *Meatballs.*

Along with Joey Bernstein and our more orthodox yet still wiseass new buddy, Gabe from Brooklyn, I made a point of trying to converse with this gentleman as he cooked up his unappealing house specialty. In broken English, our new desert rat friend asked each of us where we were from. Gabe in the *yarmulke* was quick to proudly declare, "Brooklyn," which seemed to impress the man a little. Then I attempted to explain that Joey and I both came from a place "very near New York

City." Immediately, the man seemed suspicious. "*Where* very near New York City?" he asked, *nay*, demanded.

"Well . . . it's called New Jersey, actually," I said perhaps a tad defensively.

"*New Jersey!*" the Bedouin exclaimed as he exploded in uproarious laughter and pointed repeatedly at Joey and me in the international language of pure, condescending mockery.

For the first time—from my toxic viewpoint on what I now knew was always going to be considered the wrong side of the George Washington Bridge—I felt a kind of shame and a recognition that whether I accepted it or not, my original sin was simply in hailing from the Garden State.

For almost half my life now I have lived in Los Angeles, and if you ask me, L.A.'s fine but it's not home. New Jersey's home, but it's not mine no more. Regrets, I've had a few, but then again, too few to mention. Yet in retrospect, let me make just this one exception:

In retrospect, I *really* wish I'd lied and told that bastard that I was from Brooklyn.

In 1980, Neil Diamond was asked in *Playboy* to explain why Brooklyn, New York, had produced so many celebrities. "We were indoors a lot," he said. "The weather wasn't so good. It's not as though we were on surfboards all day."

Pete Hamill—the great New York novelist, essayist, and journalist who grew up in Brooklyn just a few years before Neil Diamond—once wrote about walking down a few of his own Brooklyn roads to Ebbets Field, the legendary but now leveled home of the Dodgers, who would break hearts when they left town a half century ago.

Nobody we knew owned a car, so we went there on foot from where I lived, walking across the hills and meadows of Prospect Park. By the time we reached Flatbush Avenue, there was a convergence of all the tribes of Brooklyn: the Jews and the Irish and the Italians, immigrants and their American children; old-timers who had moved from the waterfront neighborhoods to the higher slopes to be near the great ballpark; tough lean men who had survived Iwo Jima and Anzio and the Hurtgen Forest, places where they had lost the hyphenated prefixes of origin and had become Americans; and of course, all those black Americans, including men with gray hair who had waited for too many decades to see Jack Roosevelt Robinson walk on big league grass.

Like the Brooklyn Dodgers, Neil Diamond eventually left town and headed west to Los Angeles. Diamond made his move to L.A. at the end of the sixties, perhaps yearning to play in the music industry's greener, big league grass rather than witness the slow fade of New York's Tin Pan Alley. Ever since that coastal migration, this self-professed "New York Boy," who famously proclaimed himself torn between two coasts in "I Am . . . I Said," has spent many more summers breathing the ocean breezes of Malibu than those of Coney Island.

Yet for anyone who listens at all closely, the truth remains that those Brooklyn roads Diamond so vividly recalls have never really left him or his music. As Neil once explained before breaking into "Beautiful Noise" during one of his network television specials, "You know, for as long as I can remember, I've been affected by the sounds around me, whether it be the sound of applause, or the noisy, beautiful, passionate sounds of the streets of New York City where all my songs had their roots."

Listen closely to "Brooklyn Roads"—or a lesser-known but lively number, "Brooklyn on a Saturday Night," which Diamond recorded a couple of decades later—and you can feel that the man's roots run deep. Geographically, Neil Diamond is now a true citizen of a listening world, one of a very select group of artists who needs no introduction anywhere on the world stage. Yet Diamond will always be a loving and dutiful son of New York, the world's single hottest melting pot, musically and otherwise.

The record shows that Neil Leslie Diamond was born in Brooklyn on January 24, 1941, the son of Akeeba and Rose Diamond. Two years later there came a little brother named Harvey Diamond. Despite what some might think based on "America," perhaps his most iconic song, it was not Neil himself who did the coming to America, but rather his grandparents. On the Diamond side, Akeeba, known to friends as Kieve, came here courtesy of Abram and Sadie Diamond, who had emigrated from Poland. His mother Rose's parents—Abraham and Molly Rappaport—came to America from Russia.

Years later when preparing to film *The Jazz Singer*, Diamond would write "America," a song that continues to shine a considerable light on the path so many took in search of the American Dream. Diamond has on a number of occasions named "America" as the song he's written of which he is most proud, and there can be little doubt why. In the liner notes for his *In My Lifetime* box set, Diamond described the song as being "one from the heart for my grandparents who made the journey and passed on the folklore of it to their grandchildren. I am just passing it on to my kids and theirs."

Recalling the Brooklyn of his youth to Larry King on his CNN show in 2003, Neil described Brooklyn as "a very protected environment," a separate world distinct even from nearby Manhattan. Because of World War II, however, Neil and his brother Harvey were less isolated than most sons of Brooklyn. Unlike most in their neighborhood, the Diamond boys grew up not just in Brooklyn, but also in Cheyenne, Wyoming, where from 1942 to 1945, the United States Army stationed their father during the war. Leaving behind a stationery store in Bensonhurst for more wide open spaces, and going west as such a young man with his family, appears to have profoundly shaped Diamond's eventual artistic sensibility. For a Jewish kid, Neil Diamond has long displayed impressively catholic tastes.

"I think Cheyenne had a big influence on me," Diamond explained when I first asked him about his childhood for *Rolling Stone* in 1988. "That's where I got my love of cowboys. Because I always thought I was one after I came back from Cheyenne." He was, he added with a laugh, "a Brooklyn cowboy." Later Neil said that as a teenager, "I used to take people riding at the Brooklyn Riding Academy. And I always loved the singing-cowboy movies. And on the back of comic books, there was always that ad where kids would get free gifts if you sold enough greeting cards, and my eyes always went right to that guitar—there was always a guy on a horse with a cowboy hat and a guitar."

Listen again to "Solitary Man" and you're hearing not only a song that forever defined the Diamond persona, you're hearing the first great ballad of a Brooklyn cowboy—the sound of a lonely guy riding high in the saddle on the A Train toward the bright lights of the big city. No wonder, then, that decades later, toward the end of the road on his own historic ride, Johnny Cash had no trouble at all making Diamond's "Solitary Man" his own.

Back from the service and the Wild West, the Diamonds returned east and the family set up shop in Brooklyn once again, first with a haberdashery in the East New York section. Diamond has fondly recalled his time living in Coney Island, an area that offered a young man certain tantalizing cultural advantages that he would still be able to list during a 2001 interview with British television host Gloria Hunniford: "the best hot dogs in the world, the best cotton candy and parades." Then in 1953, Kieve opened Diamond's, a dry goods store farther inland in a less breezy stretch of Flatbush. Making a living was decidedly a family affair at Diamond's. As Neil described the place on *Behind the Music*, it was a neighborhood store, one that sold such essentials as socks and underwear and, yes, bras. "Which I helped a lot of women try to fit into," Neil added with a grin.

Over the years, Neil has spoken many times of looking out at the world from inside the various Diamond family stores of his youth, suggesting that the young Brooklyn dreamer was formulating his own plan to go out and conquer the world. But in my mind, Diamond's early brush with the wonderful world of retail may have shaped his own extraordinary commercial success. After all, unlike some other of his contemporaries who are singers and songwriters, Diamond has always seemed to maintain a sense of responsibility for keeping his customers satisfied. Perhaps that's why they come back and give him their business, year after year, decade after decade.

A year later, in 1954, Neil entered Erasmus High where he was part of the mixed chorus with Streisand, with whom he sang but never spoke. Two years later, the Diamonds moved, along with their business, closer to Brooklyn's Brighton Beach. Neil began at Lincoln High School near Coney Island where he was actively involved in both choral group and fencing—likely the single most cowboylike activity he could undertake, since Lincoln shockingly did not offer a rodeo team. A tree may grow in Brooklyn, but there's not much need for cattle rustling.

According to Herb Cohen, a lifelong friend and talented fencing buddy of Neil's, the Diamonds had a warm and welcoming home, one that Cohen was convinced had left a permanent influence on Neil. "There was really love there," Cohen said. "His family was very affectionate and very loving and very emotional. And Neil reflects that." Like many who also grew up on those same Brooklyn roads, Neil's song of the same name was one of Cohen's all-time favorites. As he put it, "The song of Neil coming home, hugging his father and kissing him on his cheek and feeling his beard really touches me."

"Brooklyn Roads" remains one of Diamond's most picturesque and vivid songs, a very personal and yet most relatable recollection of youth, right from its opening lines: "If I close my eyes / I can almost hear my mother / Calling 'Neil, go find your brother.'" This is a song with a fantastically specific sense of place, from the image of two boys racing up the staircase to the apartment they lived in "two floors above the butcher / first door on the right" to "report cards I was always afraid to show." Forty years later, "Brooklyn Roads" remains a song that I've seen reduce grown men to tears, including a few times when I was looking in the mirror.

With its warm, lived-in sense of family, "Brooklyn Roads" suggested that Neil Diamond was not always a solitary man. Then again, "Solitary Man" is hardly the only song in Diamond's early cannon to suggest a certain tendency on his part to go his own way. In "Shilo," addressing a "young child with dreams" who makes up an imaginary friend, he is at least partially addressing his own younger self. The song is, as Diamond once memorably and correctly put it, "a feast for psychological interpretation." Then there's "The Boat That I Row," another persona-shaping number in the tradition of "Solitary Man." Diamond sings from the point of view of a suitor wooing a woman by telling her of his almost James Dean–like isolation: "I don't go around with the local crowd / I don't dig what's in so I guess I'm out." This was, Neil told me once, "my first rebel song."

Considering the strong, almost existential sense of loneliness at the heart of so much of Diamond's best early work, it could be surmised that he was a lonely child. But as Diamond says, "I look back at the 80mm films that my father took of me when I was a child, and I *look* as happy as any other kid. I had my parents with me, and my kid brother; when I got bored I could always beat him up. [laughs] Maybe I do have a little bit of a tendency to go off by myself and do my own thing. . . . I often wonder if anybody would ask me if I had a particularly lonely childhood if 'Solitary Man' hadn't been my first chart record. Maybe I felt solitary that day, and maybe I just liked the way the word sounded with that melody."

Nearly two decades later, Rachel Cook in the London *Observer* pursued much the same line of questioning, asking Diamond directly about the origins of his melancholia. Diamond told her that he did not know, and that he had been born that way. He said that his parents were extroverts who loved dancing. "I was the black sheep of the family, a quiet kid," Diamond explained. When Cook followed up by asking if this state of mind had improved with age, Diamond added, "It's pretty much the same. I've tried to deal with it, to get rid of it, but it's part of me at this point. I've accepted what I am. I'm content, but there's always a cloud that's hovering over me that threatens rain at any moment." This same mixture of darkness and light would eventually be well reflected in Neil Diamond's music, an expression of who he is and where he comes from, both geographically and emotionally.

Growing up in New York in the forties and fifties, Neil Diamond could hardly help but hear a wide world of music, from traditional Jewish music to more sultry Latin rhythms to big show tunes to the romantic dance music from the *Make Believe Ballroom* on WNEW to the forbidden early rumblings of the coming rock-and-roll revolution as heard on WINS during Alan Freed's *Moondog Rock 'n' Roll Party*.

As Diamond once told the Australian music writer Glenn A. Baker, "I was into every kind of music because New York really is a melting pot, with radio stations playing everything from Latin to country music to jazz." According to Neil, music had a valued place in the Diamond home, especially music to which you could dance. "My mom and dad were goers, they were doers," he recalled. "They would do anything to go dancing. Saturday night they would crash a wedding just to dance with a band." Decades before Vince Vaughn and Owen Wilson made it hip, Rose and Kieve Diamond were two of the original wedding crashers. Neil has also spoken of his parents taking him along to hear some of the great dance bands of the era, including Tito Puente's, perhaps helping to nurture their son's growing passion for rhythm.

Neil has even recalled childhood memories of his very gregarious father lip-synching "C'est Si Bon" as Eartha Kitt while wearing a costume made by Neil's mother, an image that suggests Diamond came by his own showman tendencies quite naturally. In a 1994 *Interview* article in which he was posed questions by fellow songwriter and occasional collaborator Carole Bayer Sager, Neil described his father as "an amateur performer" and added that his father's father had exhibited some of the same performing instincts. As Diamond memorably put it, "I come from a short line of hams, you know—kosher hams."

Like any other young person, Neil Diamond had his own early musical favorites, including the harmonic convergence known as the Everly Brothers—Phil and Don—the same dynamic duo that would soon inspire the teenaged John Lennon and Paul McCartney to sing together as the Foreverly Brothers.

In *Off the Record: An Oral History of Popular Music* by the famed record executive Joe Smith, Diamond recalled, "My first public performance singing was at my own bar mitzvah." There is also a charming story of a much earlier first live performance from Diamond, lip-synching to the comic opera *The Marriage of Figaro* at age three and actually winning a children's singing contest.

Still, Diamond didn't seriously consider that music might shape his path until 1956, when he spent some quality leftie time in the country during a winter reunion of childhood campers at Surprise Lake Camp, a progressive Jewish camp about sixty miles north of Manhattan in Cold Spring, New York, whose other distinguished camping alumni include Eddie Cantor, Walter Matthau, Jerry Stiller, Larry King, and Gene Simmons of Kiss.

"It was a very liberal camp," Diamond recalled to me in *Rolling Stone*. "We went for a winter get-together at Surprise Lake, and Pete Seeger came up and played for us. Some of the kids played their songs for him, and they were all singing about causes, you know, whatever causes meant something to a fourteen-year-old. That was the first time I realized that my peers could write songs. And that I could do it too, maybe, just for fun. Not thinking that, *hey*, this could be my life." It was there at the camp, he added in our *Behind the Music* interview, where "I was exposed to lots of music and it kind of inspired me to take guitar lessons and learn how to play."

The public relations department at Neil's early label, Bang, tried to romanticize Diamond's upbringing a bit by suggesting that as a young man he had formed an a cappella group called the Memphis Backstreet Boys and run away from home. Not exactly the sort of thing a nice boy from a good family in the dry goods trade would ever try. "That biography was made up by the folks at Bang," he told me in *Rolling Stone*. "I think they wanted to make up a fascinating history for Neil Diamond. See, what they wanted was more like a Bob Dylan or a Van Morrison, you know? But what they got was a Jewish kid from Brooklyn, and they didn't think that was interesting. And so they made something up." Like that great line from *The Man Who Shot Liberty Valance* puts it, "When the legend becomes fact, print the legend."

The actual facts are that Neil Diamond enrolled at Lincoln High School in 1956 where he seemed to flourish, despite a very mixed academic record until then. "I moved my senior year," Diamond told Larry King in 2003. "It was the best thing that ever happened to me, moving to Lincoln, because Erasmus was a very tough school. It was an inner-city kind of a school. And Lincoln was like the movie *Grease*, you know, with the kids all dancing."

Diamond may not have been dancing all that much at Lincoln, but along with his new friend and fencing team captain, Herb Cohen, he found himself fencing on the school team, perhaps following in the grand tradition of one of his early heroes, Cyrano de Bergerac, whom Neil has called "a misfit . . . a great swordsman . . . a poet"—which sounds very much like a nice piece of literary self-analysis. Neil proved to be a real natural at his chosen sport. In his first and only year at Lincoln, the school's fencing team won a surprise championship in the New York City scholastic fencing competition. Years later, Diamond would speak of how his success in fencing made him feel like a winner for the first time. Eventually, again with Cohen's support, fencing would also earn Diamond a scholarship to New York University, where he intended to start the long process of becoming a doctor, the sine qua non of countless Jewish parents in Brooklyn and many other locations in the known universe.

Dr. Neil Diamond was not to be, ultimately because Neil was at the same time lunging forward with another growing passion that would soon come to transform his life—the overwhelming desire to make music. Diamond's progress in music would be more gradual than in fencing. In January of 1957, he was given his first secondhand guitar for his sixteenth birthday, and before long he was spending many hours downstairs in the Diamond family basement playing away on a guitar or an old player piano, making his own kind of music for the first time.

Beyond his fundamental desire to express himself, Diamond's new musical drive may have been a fortunate matter of location, location, location, and a healthy sense of competition with another Neil who was already making a very big impression at Lincoln High, and soon enough far beyond the insular world of Brooklyn.

"Neil Sedaka had a very big impact on me," Diamond told Joe Smith in *Off the Record*. "My senior year I went to Lincoln High School, and Sedaka was at Lincoln, and he was a professional singer. He had records out and you could hear them on the radio. Back then, you judged yourself against Sedaka."

Somewhere inside of him, Diamond must have had the confidence or the intuition to believe that he could rise to that level. And so it was that, after an introduction from his brother, Harvey, Neil got together with a new friend named Jack Parker from around the corner who was much more of a trained vocalist. As Diamond would later recall to Smith, the pair would rehearse in his basement attempting to be the Everly Brothers, "which is hard if you're from Brooklyn."

Still, before long, with the help of his loving parents, Neil would score his first non–bar mitzvah gig when he and Jack played a dinner dance at the Little Neck Country Club, a world away in Long Island. This was not exactly the kind of high-profile gig to put Neil Sedaka on notice that there was a new Neil in town. Yet it was a beginning, a first step down a long road that would not be an easy one.

When he graduated Lincoln High in June of 1958, Neil Leslie Diamond was hardly alone traveling down those Brooklyn roads in an attempt to get to the top of the pops, one way or another. Nor was Neil Diamond's remarkable generation of musical dreamers even the first to dare to travel beyond the Brooklyn Bridge and try and make a little musical history.

When I asked him once to theorize on why so many significant and successful sixties pop stars came out of just a few Brooklyn high schools, Diamond said this: "Every school kid in Brooklyn learns at some point that George Gershwin was born in Brooklyn and that he became a very respected musical prodigy around the world. So there was a tradition there. Also there just happened to be a couple of teenage geniuses who lived in Brooklyn then. It was like a little clique there, people competing with each other. Sedáka came back and played my high school, and he was great. But why Brooklyn?

"First of all, I think it was a way to get out."

Song Sung 3

STREET LIFE

Say boy, you got to get street-wise
Hey, little boy, you're a babe in arms
Stay out of harm's way

—"STREET LIFE," BY NEIL DIAMOND

NOT THAT ANY OF YOU BOTHERED TO ASK, BUT I WAS BORN IN THE since-condemned French Hospital in New York City on December 16, 1961. Historians will long remember this as a date which will live in infamy since it marks the precise beginning of the end for a species of real man that immediately preceded my generation that I like to call the Kick-Ass American Jew.

Rich Cohen, who's a tougher Jew than me, has written an interesting book about "Tough Jews," a particularly pugnacious subsection of these Kick-Ass American Jews of whom I speak and from whom I am proudly descended. Compared to actual, potentially ass-kicking Tough Jews, the Kick-Ass American Jews were marked less by a shared toughness than a tenacious tendency to succeed well beyond any reasonable expectations, and in many cases, beyond even the unreasonable expectations of their own Jewish immigrant parents.

As Neil Diamond said of his own parents, my parents' generation was a group of true "goers and doers" on their way to becoming movers and shakers. Like some sort of new Semitic renaissance, this generation went out and did groundbreaking, productive, and profitable work in law, in medicine, in business, in the arts—even in the occasional sport, like that elusive Brooklyn-turned-Los-Angeles-Dodger Sandy Koufax. In short, these men and women kicked some *serious* American ass. Some of them, like my own father, also found some time as young men to kick ass on foreign soil and win a world war.

This greatest Jewish generation—achieving so much, so fast in the shadow of the Holocaust—grew up mostly in close quarters in and around New York City and other major American urban centers. They worked their asses off at outstanding public schools, skipping grades at will, then made their own way through college and sometimes grad school. Then they went out, got married, and, two by two, took over much of our world—one good job and nice suburban home full of Ben Shahn paintings and Philip Roth books at a time. And so it was that the Kick-Ass American Jews made their immigrant parents proud and, in remarkable numbers, made their mark too.

Okay, now let's take a turn for the worse and talk about *my* generation.

You might remember us. We're those spoiled bums who were raised in relative affluence in the suburbs, sent to the finest of schools, both public and private. We were then handed every opportunity to freely pursue our varied interests, sent off to the colleges of our choice where we joined co-ops or those frats and sororities that would *never* have admitted our parents. Without the enormous pressure to succeed, some of us grew fat, lazy, and even bohemian. When we screwed up, which we did frequently, we did so knowing full well that Mom and Dad would most likely be there to bail us out and ensure that we'd always know from where our next bong or futon was coming. We were too young to be drafted into the war in Viet Nam, but would likely have proven just as useless in wartime as we were in peace. Some of us managed to become semiproductive members of society despite all of our many advantages. Others rejected or quite simply managed to blow all the many chances handed to us on a silver platter and went, as my Brooklyn-born-and-raised father-in-law memorably put it to me once, "from coolie to coolie" in just two generations.

Consider this generational devolution in a microcosm.

My father grew up without a father or any money, bouncing around a series of New York public schools that were, admittedly, the best in the world, including the illustrious Bronx School of Science from which he graduated. When he wasn't in school, my dad would bounce around a series of small apartments that he, his Romanian pogrom-fleeing immigrant mother, and two little sisters would share—fleeing frequently in the middle of the night when the rent was due. Exactly what my crazy and wonderful grandmother did to make money and support those three kids during what is too sweetly dubbed the Great Depression has been a matter of no small speculation behind closed doors. But at this late date, without checking the statute of limitations, we will choose to assume it was legal.

Somehow in this chaotic context, my brilliant father managed to take possession of some empty tenement hall closet and use it for a series of science experiments that would win a New York City public school contest. Hearing of this remarkable triumph, my father's dentist—who must have had an unusually big heart for someone in his chosen profession—took an interest in Dad's further education. He took the time to help this kid with precious little support anywhere in the world get a partial scholarship to his own Ivy League alma matter, Cornell University.

So it was that my father would attend and ultimately graduate Cornell while working multiple jobs, including waiting tables, and keeping the boiler of a fancy fraternity going in frigid Ithaca, New York, in exchange for sleeping for free in a spare room. Not only did this son of an uneducated Romanian immigrant effectively earn his way through Cornell, he managed at the same time to send money home to support his mother and two little sisters back in the city. He wanted to be a doctor, a process that would become forever interrupted by another little challenge—going off to become a Jewish naval officer and successfully surviving World War II.

For comparison's sake, with the exception of coping poorly with the emotional aftermath of my parent's eventual ugly and lengthy divorce, I was raised not unlike a veal—a particularly spoiled and well-fed veal with an unusually large allowance—and went off to prep school and then Cornell (as a legacy) without any great desire to become a man or much of anything else.

Neil Diamond went off to college at New York University to become a doctor, to heal others, to become a great fencer and take on all comers with his confident thrust and parry, and perhaps become a great musical artist.

I went off to Cornell without a clue or a driver's license, still hoping very much to get laid.

One of us would go on to graduate.

The other would drop out of college.

One of us would go on to make music history.

The other would, with considerable difficulty, *eventually* learn how to make lunch.

One of us would marry quite young and write "Solitary Man."

The other would write very little of note and, for the worse part of a decade, remain a solitary and horny man.

Which of us, you wonder rhetorically, was which?

You do the math, because math was never one of my better subjects.

The summer before they would both start college at New York University, two good-looking and agile young Jewish pals from Brooklyn—Neil Diamond and Herb Cohen—did something considerably more predictable than thrust and parry in competitive fencing. They headed for the hills, the Catskills namely, to try and earn a few extra dollars for their upcoming freshman year. It was·while waiting up there in the hills, safely transporting brisket and other potentially explosive staples of the Catskills nondiet, that Neil Diamond would meet the woman who would not only inspire his first notable song, but also become his first wife.

Her name was Jay Posner, and by all accounts she was a lovely young lady from a good family in Long Island. Posner was herself headed to study at Hofstra University with the intention of becoming a schoolteacher, an admirable and far from uncommon career choice for the women of her generation. "Teaching is what women did back then, at least until we got married," my mother, Carol, a former New York public school teacher herself, once explained to me.

Clearly impressed with Jay—or Jaye, as she preferred—Neil Diamond would woo his first great love with a very sweet, very yearning, very fifties-sounding love song entitled "Hear Them Bells," a derivative yet exceedingly charming doo-wop-inspired number that Neil would much later revisit in concert during the early nineties.

"Hear Them Bells" sounds as if it could have been a minor hit for an act like Dion and the Belmonts or Danny and the Juniors and figures very prominently in Diamond's early musical history. Neil Diamond identified "Hear Them Bells" this way: "This is my first song. There's no demo because at that time I didn't even know what a demo was." In his introduction to his box set, he remembered wondering after he'd written "Hear Them Bells" if his first song "was an accident or a trick or possibly something more."

At the time, Diamond simply explained that "Hear Them Bells" was written "for a girlfriend." Five years later, he was more forthcoming about the fact that the girlfriend for whom he wrote these romantic lines—"I'll be yours forever, sweetheart / Our love is real, we'll never ever part"—and who made him hear bells was in fact his future first wife.

"I really wanted to impress her and I couldn't afford to buy her a gift," Diamond explained. "So I wrote a song called 'Hear Them Bells' and basically it was a song saying, you know, 'Will you marry me?'" And it worked. The two were soon inseparable, even if it meant a few train rides to see her with her family in Massapequa, Long Island.

Beyond finding the first significant love of his life, and the eventual mother of his first two children, Diamond apparently made one less meaningful and pleasant connection at Fun Crest. According to *Diamond*, an unauthorized 1987 biography written by Alan Grossman, Bill Truman, and Roy Oki Yamanaka, Neil also spent some time at Fun Crest getting advice from the veteran entertainers who played the hotel. He was informed that to make it in show business, he needed an agent. Not yet the savvy music business professional that he would eventually become, Diamond reportedly signed a seven-year deal with a saxophonist who promised to score the young hopeful gigs in exchange for 50 percent of Neil's then-imaginary musical income. Later, Diamond's father would give him $750 to buy himself out of this bad deal. This would turn out to be the first, but not the last time that Neil would bet on himself professionally and win big.

Diamond was soon winning on yet another front, performing admirably with the Violets, the New York University fencing team, and in the process greatly impressing his coach, Hugo Castello. Castello was a legendary figure in the sport who would ultimately coach New York University to ten national championships, two of them while

Neil was his third man in sabre. Yet even with extraordinary success in this sport of kings, there were signs that Diamond's heart was not in being third man in sabre as much as it was in trying to be first man in song.

"He used to bring his guitar on our road trips and play in the back while all the guys were playing cards and stuff; he would sing for us," Herb Cohen says. In *Diamond*, Coach Castello is quoted recalling about his famous former fencer, "Once in two consecutive duel meets, he didn't have a touch scored against him. I think that's still a school record."

Yet, increasingly, it was the prospect of making records and writing songs that took up more and more of Diamond's time. Beyond the occasional performance with Jack Packer, Neil started to record demos of the songs that he was writing on his Wollensack reel-to-reel tape recorder, learning his first lessons in the art of recording along the way. Decades later, Diamond would decide to share some of these early demos on the *In My Lifetime* compilation. One listen is enough to know that Diamond's breakthrough song was his fifth effort: a dramatic ballad from 1958 called "Blue Destiny" that sounds heavily influenced by the Everly Brothers' best songs of that era. Here, for the first time, we can see the promising first glimmers of the gift and the persona that would emerge fully on "Solitary Man" eight long years later.

Like "Solitary Man," "Blue Destiny" is a vaguely haunting tune written from the perspective of a man who has been romantically wronged and is trying to figure out his place in this world. "This was the first song that had an emotional effect on me," Diamond explained in the liner notes for *In My Lifetime*. "For me it had a uniqueness and an honesty that made me feel as though I could be a real writer at some point."

"At some point" felt as if it could not come soon enough for Diamond, as it became increasingly clear that his heart was more in midtown's Tin Pan Alley than downtown on campus at N.Y.U. where he was attempting to compete not only in fencing, but also in a premed program that was becoming more and more challenging. In his 2003 interview with Larry King, Diamond opened up about both his motivation in wanting to be a doctor and the reason this perhaps more seemingly respectable career choice was not to be. Diamond spoke of losing a grandmother to cancer and his desire to find a cure for the disease. Then, as Diamond confessed, "Along the way I met reality, which was organic chemistry." It was around that time When Neil Met Organic Chemistry that music or even business school suddenly started looking like a much better idea to him.

As the sixties dawned for Neil Diamond, he sought to find his own musical identity while watching Neil Sedaka run up a series of big hits, starting with "The Diary" in 1958, and continuing with pop smashes like "Oh Carol" in 1959, "Calendar Girl" in 1960, "Happy Birthday Sweet Sixteen" in 1961, and "Breaking Up Is Hard to Do" in 1962.

Then Carole Klein would become Carole King and find her own foot in the door of the Brill Building with a cloying but not entirely unsuccessful novelty answer record to Sedaka's "Oh Carol" called—what else?—"Oh Neil." At Queens College, she would get to know not only Paul Simon but also her future husband and songwriter collaborator, Gerry Goffin. In the fifties, the very concept of the teenager took hold in the media, and soon not only were teens being marketed to, prodigies like Sedaka and King were selling this new teen dream to their own generation in song.

As Carole King saw it, going from Brooklyn to the Brill Building wasn't an unimaginable leap. As she pointed out in the excellent documentary *The Hit Makers: The Teens Who Stole Pop Music*, "We were a subway ride away from Manhattan—the hub of all this sort of thing, which it still is. So it was so possible. For a kid living in Dubuque, Iowa, it's a much longer journey."

Diamond saw what was happening not from Dubuque, but rather from his frustratingly close vantage point downtown at N.Y.U. He watched with great interest as a pack of future "gods," young songwriters mostly from Brooklyn, started to make names for themselves as a new generation of tunesmiths on Tin Pan Alley. Al Nevins' and Don Kirshner's Aldon Music—founded during Diamond's freshman year and based around the Brill Building at 1619 Broadway, just north of Times Square—became the new epicenter of New York's music publishing world. Suddenly, the Brill Building and a few nearby offices were the place to be if you wanted to be part of pop music's new pantheon.

"There really was this hustle and bustle of creativity and activity," is how Ellie Greenwich recalled the period to me for Neil Diamond's *Behind the Music*. "Rock and roll was a baby, and you were actually part of the growing process, and it was very exciting."

Only forty or so blocks south of this dream world, Diamond could be forgiven for feeling so close yet so far away. Unfortunately, his own first recording efforts were considerably less successful. Keeping up with that other, better known Neil was looking more and more difficult.

Then in 1960, Neil Diamond and Jack Packer signed as a singing duo to Allied Entertainment Corporation of America, associated with a publishing concern called Saxon Music Corp, and even released Neil & Jack's first single with the ultra-Everly Brotherly-sounding "What Will I Do" on the A side, and a less rocking number called "You Are My Love at Last" on the flip. Reportedly, some DJs decided to play the flip side, but mostly radio chose to simply ignore Neil & Jack entirely. Even Neil himself has never spoken that highly of this first single— though he has mentioned that he quite enjoyed the fact that Duel Record, the company that released it, was a subsidiary of Shell Records and Gulf Records, whose record labels read: "Shell Records and Gulf Records, our records are a gas."

The early live performances of Neil & Jack were by some accounts less than the total gas one might have hoped for. Jack Packer's less than rave review of the style of the man on the other side of that ampersand has been repeated often, including in a 2006 piece in the *New Yorker* on Diamond. Onstage, young Neil, Packer once said, was "very uptight, to say the least. Somber. I realized that performing per se was not his forte whatsoever." With all due respect to Neil's first important musical collaborator, by the time his classic live album *Hot August Night* was released in 1972, Neil Diamond would establish himself as one of the most charismatic and crowd-pleasing performers of his generation. As for Jack Packer—not so much.

In the 1987 biography *Neil Diamond: Solitary Star*, Jack Packer told author Rich Wiseman that he and Neil's first recording session was much more of a gas than their live appearances. "Like the first time you have sex" was how he memorably put it. Neil & Jack would experience a few other brushes with success, and barely release another single ("I'm Afraid" backed with "Till You've Tried Love") during the next year or so, but by 1962 Neil Diamond was a solitary act again, at least professionally.

It was around the same time that Neil Diamond made a number of decisions that would forever change his life. He would leave New York University only thirteen credits shy of graduation in order to give music his full attention. Unsurprisingly perhaps, this was *not* a decision that he would rush to share with his parents, though he has often stressed that he knew that his mother and father were always very much "in my corner."

After hustling his songs around Tin Pan Alley, Diamond had received what he has called "an office I couldn't refuse"—a gig as an apprentice songwriter for Sunbeam Music, a small publishing company, earning $50 a week. Diamond took the job, and decided not long after to marry Jaye, who was now teaching in the city. For a short time, the new Mr. and Mrs. Diamond would move back into his parents' home so that he could afford to pursue his musical mission, with the financial help of Jaye's more steady teaching salary. By late 1962, Neil and Jaye's first daughter, Marjorie, was born, and one can only imagine the pressures the young couple must have been feeling to try and make their own home and find a way to pay for it. In the book *Diamond*, Neil is quoted as saying, "I married as a child at twenty . . . it took courage to live the way we did."

As he made a series of such nervy choices, Diamond was excited but also very concerned. "I had no idea how I could make a living and have a family while being a musician or a songwriter, but it was something I loved," Neil told me. To borrow a phrase from one of the better and more confessional songs that he would write in this period, Diamond was feeling a bit like a "straw in the wind" as he cast his fate and the fate of his young family to the wind to pursue a long shot of a dream.

Diamond told me once that "Straw in the Wind" was written with the now Belmont-less Dion DiMucci in mind, and this rhythmic number would indeed have sounded convincing coming from the man who gave the world "The Wanderer." In a sign of more frustrating times to come, Diamond would get as far as personally pitching the song to Dion on a bench in Central Park, the singer's chosen meeting spot. Ultimately, Dion would turn down the song, but what Diamond stressed was that this major recording artist he admired had offered him encouragement to go on and write more.

Here, in his early struggles to make his name and even make a decent living, we see the confidence and the character that would ultimately allow Neil Diamond to become the sort of superstar he gradually transformed himself into. Though it was likely he felt not unlike that straw in the wind, that central belief in his own self-worth would ultimately prove to be unshakeable and entirely well deserved. Yet, as much as he may have felt that his dream would come true eventually, he could not have known what would happen to him as he boldly left behind his studies downtown to try his luck full time in music's new Tin Pan Alley.

At this point, Diamond's dream was less to become the next Dion than to get office work as one of those well-paid gods in the cubicles working for weekly salaries at the Brill Building and turning out hit after hit for others. "I didn't think being a professional singer on records was something that was in the future for me," he recalled to me for *In My Lifetime* liner notes. "That was beyond anything I could imagine."

School was out for Diamond now, but there were many more lessons still to learn.

In the very best tradition of the Ass-Kicking American Jews before him, Neil Diamond was taking his shot. But before he could take his rightful place, he would have to get his own ass kicked first.

SOLITARY MAN SEEKS OFFICE WORK

I've had it to here bein' where love's a small word
Part-time thing, paper ring

—"SOLITARY MAN," BY NEIL DIAMOND

CHET ATKINS—THE LEGENDARILY WISE AND WONDERFUL GUITARIST, producer, and record executive with whom Neil Diamond would record the song "Blue Highway" on his 1996 album *Tennessee Moon*—once said that "a long apprenticeship is the most logical way to success. The only alternative is overnight stardom, but I can't give you a formula for that."

Neil Diamond has been so extraordinarily successful for so long now that it seems almost impossible to imagine a time when he struggled to survive in the music business. To meet Diamond today is to shake hands with an American institution, one of obvious global value. After all, Neil Diamond has been a popular brand name for more than four decades now, and he consistently remains one of the biggest live draws in the international concert industry.

Yet struggle Diamond did for much of the first half of the sixties, as he served his extended musical apprenticeship by knocking around midtown Manhattan trying to make enough noise to get truly noticed in the fast-changing world of Tin Pan Alley. In his liner notes to *Up on the Roof: Songs from the Brill Building*, Diamond described Tin Pan Alley as being "about six square blocks of Manhattan filled with music publishing companies, managers, agents, recording agents, recording studios and swarms of other songwriters, people just like me with whom I could share the agony and also the sheer fun of the music business."

For all the agony he would live through and all the fun he would enjoy while surviving the life of a struggling singer and songwriter, the apprenticeship of Neil Diamond would turn out to be longer than he had perhaps imagined. But in the end, it would not be wasted time at all. The lessons that Diamond learned early on would shape all the far more golden and platinum years that would follow. Yet in the beginning, that initial offer of a mere $50-a-week job as an apprentice songwriter for Sunbeam Music was enough for Diamond to make his move.

"I was still writing terrible songs, very sophomoric," Neil told me, "but I could say honestly that I was a songwriter."

I once asked him to describe the Tin Pan Alley scene that he found when he first arrived there. "Everyone wanted one of those geniuses," Neil said, going on to name many of the songwriting legends of the Brill Building, pronouncing each name with obvious respect. Speaking of all these resident songwriting gods, Diamond appeared to be very much including himself when he noted, "Everyone wanted to be like them and to write as well as them. Together they probably had more of an effect on American contemporary music than anybody. So that's what you aspired to."

Diamond would aspire, and almost certainly perspire, a great deal over the next few years of agony and ecstasy. That apprentice songwriting gig with Sunbeam Music would end after only sixteen weeks without one of Neil's songs being covered. Asked about his first song-writing job by Larry King on CNN in 2003, Diamond remembered, "I submitted some audition songs, a bunch of songs that I'd written. They were all beginners' songs. But rock-and-roll really was in its in-fancy then, and they didn't know." Diamond explained that his pub-lisher was mostly a Broadway show publisher, but that with the changing of the guard going on in music then, they were looking to expand their horizons, particularly if it only cost them $50 a week. "They wanted to get into this new field called rock-and-roll," Dia-mond told King. "And here I was, a kid. I was stupid. You know, I would work for nothing. And so they signed me."

Before long, Sunbeam would drop Diamond too. And so over the next few years, Neil would hustle to score a number of similar jobs for a succession of mostly small publishing concerns with only a little more success than he first found at Sunbeam Music.

Increasingly, as a wave of hopeful young writers continued to come and storm the Brill Building, inspired by high-profile success stories like Sedaka and King, the competition for covers and airplay grew ever more intense. Beneath the level of the young Brill Building legends, Diamond pointed out, there were many other writers to knock out a hit. These writers were, he pointed out, "young, middle-aged, old and leftover from different periods—all trying to have their music heard."

Diamond experienced most of the Brill Building era from an ever-so-slight distance. As he put it in his gracious notes for *Up on the Roof: Songs from the Brill Building*, "I was in the waiting room while they were being written inside, often by people from my neighborhood, sometimes even my school. Therefore, anything was possible for me."

To make the possible that much more probable, Diamond worked on multiple fronts, as a singer as well as a songwriter. One early Diamond copyright was covered by a group memorably called the Rocky Fellers, a quintet of four Filipino brothers and their dad that would have a sizable hit with "Killer Joe," but not with Neil's Latin-tinged Christmas number "Santa Santa," which is said to have done better in the Philippines.

In 1962, Diamond would ever so briefly strike a deal to record a single for a far better known record company that would figure very prominently in his future: Columbia Records. With the help of staff producer Al Kasha (who would go on to cowrite "The Morning After," the smash hit from the disaster movie classic *The Poseidon Adventure*) and product manager Tom Cantalano (who would go on to produce many of Diamond's greatest hits), Neil scored a one-off single deal with the label he would much later call home.

Backed vocally by the Angels, who later rode high with "My Boyfriend's Back," Diamond recorded "At Night" as the A side and a song called "Clown Time" on the flip side. His own best critic, Diamond offered an extremely accurate review of "At Night" in the liner notes for *In My Lifetime*: "That was me trying to be Neil Sedaka on the "A" side. And not even coming close." As for "Clown Time," Diamond noted that he included the rarity on his box set only because "the lyric was written in sociology class." He noted that he got a C in the course and would give himself just about the same grade for the song.

The record suggests that Diamond took an opportunity wherever he could find it. In 1962, he and a group of other struggling writers from Roosevelt Music Company actually banded together to write a very funny country-tinged, heartbreak song entitled "Ten Lonely Guys." Pat Boone would cover the song and take it ever so close to the top forty, peaking at #45 in the wake of Boone's greater chart triumph with "Speedy Gonzales."

Over the years, some have insisted on portraying Neil Diamond as having a serious and even somber presence. As recently as 2006, in a piece titled "Hello Again: Neil Diamond's Long, Serious Career," *New Yorker* writer Sasha Frere-Jones wrote, presumably with a straight face, "Nothing is funny in Neil Diamond's songs." Here is proof to the contrary, many years before other, better-known musical rib-ticklers like "The Non-conformist Marching Song," "Crunchy Granola Suite," or "Lonely Lady #17." At the time Diamond collaborated with the other writers on "Ten Lonely Guys," he did so under the name Mark Lewis. Diamond was far less shy in 1993 when he included a sly and loving version of this old composition alongside much better known classics of the era on *Up on the Roof: Songs from the Brill Building*.

Then again, as he struggled to make a living in music, not everything was so damn funny. Beyond the minimal salaries, Diamond has said that his big payday during his hungry years was for another funny little tune called "Measles," which earned him something like $200. Despite its memorable lyrics about being "covered with little red spots" but really having "a case of the blues," the song did not become the smash that Diamond so needed, apparently because the tune wasn't, he would joke, "contagious" enough.

Ultimately, Neil Diamond would write many big hits for both himself and others too, yet the fundamental truth learned during his apprenticeship was that he wrote first and best for Neil Diamond, and the more that his songs sounded like him and no one else, the better off he was.

While Diamond has spoken of himself as being a second-rater in the Brill Building era, Ellie Greenwich has a different view. "He was an entity unto himself," she says. "I feel badly that he feels he was a loser in that era, because I don't think he was *in* it."

Whether he was inside or out, Diamond may have benefited from a willingness to listen and learn. As he said in retrospect of those who rejected his early efforts during an interview with famed *Los Angeles*

Times rock critic Robert Hilburn that aired on *Midnight Special* in 1981, "I thought that they were right. I thought their criticism of the songs was right, and I was a beginner and I was just learning and it wasn't discouraging at all."

To make the challenge in front of him even more daunting, Diamond found himself in the position of trying to hit what was becoming a rapidly moving cultural target. As the young singer-songwriter tried his best to write popular music, dramatic shifts were occurring all around him. Bob Dylan, emerging from New York's downtown folk scene, would forever change the language of popular music with a potent blend of modern poetry and the generational politics of songs like "The Times They Are a-Changin'," "Maggie's Farm," and "It's Alright, Ma (I'm Only Bleeding)." And from across the pond came another equally fab revolution. To a nation reeling from the assassination of John F. Kennedy, Beatlemania brought a much-needed sense of joy. A Tin Pan Alley that was only just beginning to adjust to its own new titans of teen was now further threatened by a brave new world of artists and bands who could write songs for themselves, or at least *thought* they could.

"That whole interplay was very simplistic at the beginning, because rock & roll was very simplistic," Neil told me in *Rolling Stone* in 1988. "But then things became more complicated when people like Bob Dylan and John Kennedy came along. Suddenly the child-like nature of the music coming out of that area had an opportunity to change and grow."

In such a fast-changing context, it could get hard to know what music would find favor in the marketplace. Diamond has recalled listening to two songwriters working next to him who were writing very traditional Jewish-sounding songs, and thinking that his neighbors' music was going nowhere fast. Those two songwriters turned out to be

Jerry Block and Sheldon Harnick, and those more traditional tunes they were writing were for a show that opened in the fall of 1964 called *Fiddler on the Roof*. And so "If I Were a Rich Man" would be making waves well before "Solitary Man."

After John, Paul, George, and Ringo hit America and played *The Ed Sullivan Show* that same year, Diamond explained to me, "Things changed almost completely, because only those writers who were performing their own music had a chance at having their music heard. And a lot of people were kind of lost for a number of years. I think the thing that saved me is that I had no hits at that point. So I was an unknown factor."

Finding himself not only unknown, but also unsigned to either a publishing contract or a record deal, Neil Diamond bet on himself, as he would do again and again in his lifetime. Those small office cubicles where so many other songwriting duos worked happily had never really suited his style. "Well, it sure didn't work for me," he told me. "I was always conscious that people were listening to what I was doing. Now, of course, I realize that they couldn't care *less* what I was doing. So usually I did my writing at home or on the subway, anywhere but at an office."

That was, until Diamond decided with impressive confidence not to pack it in, but rather to create more suitably solitary surroundings of his own. For the princely sum of about $40 a month, he sublet a small storeroom above the famed jazz club Birdland from a printer. The place was tiny, with room enough only for a small piano, a small desk, and, in a frequently repeated story, a pay phone that Diamond somehow arranged to have put in so that he would not run up any big phone bills he could little afford. This working environment suited Diamond more than all those cubicles around the corner where people usually worked in pairs and where the bosses often asked tunesmiths to write songs to order.

"I lived in that room for a year," Diamond told me in *Rolling Stone.* "And there—for the first time working without some kind of specification about what I could write—I wrote some of the best songs I had written up to that point."

Asked why he thought that he was happier working alone in a room of one's own, Diamond answered with a laugh. "It's not like I had a lot of people beating down my door to work with me. But yes, most of what I did, I did on my own. I guess that's part of who I am."

Success did not come overnight to Neil Diamond, not by a long shot. Compared to some of his contemporaries and former schoolmates, the now twenty-five-year-old Diamond could even be considered something of a straggler, an underachiever of sorts, at least relatively speaking. Finally, though, when his extended Tin Pan Alley apprenticeship had been well served and then some, success came all the same and in servings greater than he could have imagined.

The crucial break that Neil had been looking everywhere for at long last occurred when, in February 1965, a few new, improved songs struck a chord with veteran music publishers George and Irwin Pincus during a visit to their offices. Their interest was such that they offered to pay for Diamond to record a couple of demo versions of his tunes. Remarkably, when she wasn't otherwise engaged writing pop hit after pop hit, Ellie Greenwich would also manage to squeeze in time to add her distinctive vocals on the demos for other less fortunate songwriters, which meant just about everyone else. And so it was that Diamond first met the extremely gifted woman who would do so much to finally bring him to prominence.

To Diamond, Ellie Greenwich, despite being only a couple of months older than him, was already a resident genius and one of the true goddesses of the popular song. "I would have given a toe to have written one song as good as some of the things that they were just knocking out," is how Neil put it.

Working with her husband, Jeff Barry, and sometimes with Phil Spector, Greenwich had already helped give birth to some of the most infectious pop tunes ever recorded, including all-time classics like "Be My Baby" and "Baby, I Love You," "(And) Then He Kissed Me," "Da Doo Ron Ron," "Do Wah Diddy Diddy," and "Chapel of Love," to name a few of the more well-known gems. More recently, while working for songwriting legends Jerry Leiber and Mike Stoller's Trio Music publishing company, Barry and Greenwich had written, with George "Shadow" Morton, the number one hit motorcycle opera *Leader of the Pack,* further proof of their leading place in the current pop establishment.

To Greenwich, this Diamond guy seemed cute, quiet, and full of potential. "I thought he was adorable," she says. "And I wanted to take him home for milk and cookies; that's exactly how I felt about Neil— that you really wanted to take care of Neil, and know that when he was taken care of, he would take care of you."

"We met, we laughed, we kibitzed," Diamond told me in his *Behind the Music* interview. "And when we finished she said, 'You know, I'd like you to meet my husband. I think we could make some records with you.'"

A few weeks later, Jeff Barry agreed to find time to meet Diamond and came away a fan not just of Neil's songs but even more so of his voice. Though their own marriage was in the process of falling apart, Barry and Greenwich both decided that they would work together with this up-and-comer. So with the lobbying of his new, more powerful friends, Diamond was offered what looked like far and away his most prestigious temporary job yet—a three-month publishing deal with Leiber and Stoller's Trio Music during which he would earn $150 a week, with the additional possibility of actually doing some recording for their label, Red Bird Records.

Yet even here, among a few of the gods he worshipped, Diamond felt somehow separate. When I asked him about working as a staff writer for Leiber and Stoller in *Rolling Stone*, Diamond told me, "I hardly saw them. They were always in their room and very apart from the writers. They were writing Drifters songs. What do they want to know about some jerk with a guitar? *Nobody* wrote with a guitar in New York. It was all piano writers. So when I walked in with a guitar, I was like a hayseed, despite the fact that I was from Brooklyn."

Within a few months of losing his gig at Trio Music in June of 1965, Diamond, along with Barry and Greenwich, formed a new entity called Tallyrand Music, Inc., set up to both publish Diamond's songs and produce and exploit his own recordings. Used to being fired from other music publishers, Diamond was now president of Tallyrand and drew a $150-a-week advance from the future royalties he hoped to earn.

After years of frustrating misses, the momentum suddenly started to shift in 1965, and things actually began going Diamond's way. "Sunday and Me," a charming, catchy number that Diamond had written at Trio Music, was recorded by Jay & the Americans at the urging of Leiber and Stoller. It would hit #18 on the *Billboard* charts at the end of the year, marking Neil's first-ever top-forty hit. Though the group's performance of the song was somewhat overwrought, listen closely to the composition underneath and you can hear a strong hint of the appealing new Neil Diamond sound to come.

Diamond was now a man making his move. There would be no returning to New York University for business school now that his big opportunity in the music business had finally knocked. Seemingly putting everything on the line, Neil and Jaye moved into a house in

Massapequa, Long Island, that would be home to their first child now on the way.

Looking to make their new deal work out for everyone involved, Barry and Greenwich took Diamond to see Jerry Wexler, the famed producer and then vice president of Atlantic Records, who was impressed enough to seriously consider signing Neil to the label that had brought the world the likes of Ray Charles, Bobby Darin, and countless others. Ultimately, however, Diamond's new recording home would be shifted to a new subsidiary of Atlantic called Bang Records that had been started by Bert Berns, a former staff producer at Atlantic, whose countless credits as a songwriter and producer included work with the Isley Brothers, Solomon Burke, the Drifters, and Wilson Pickett.

In 1965, Berns formed Bang—named, it was said, by taking the first letter of his name, along with those of Atlantic's Ahmet Ertegun, his brother Neshui Ertegun, and Gerald Wexler, more commonly known as Jerry.

Before long, this upstart record company would help bring the world the McCoys ("Hang On Sloopy") and the Strangeloves ("I Want Candy"). And though Bang would fade eventually, the label lives on in music history for launching not only Diamond's career with a stunning series of hits, but also the early American career of former Them front man Van Morrison from Ireland, who would release the classic "Brown Eyed Girl" on Bang not long after Diamond's big recording debut. These two great singer-songwriters would meet up again much later, when they both played with the Band on *The Last Waltz* and became two unlikely stars in a Martin Scorsese movie.

Finally, Neil Diamond was about to get his first great shot on Bang, one that it seemed could not miss. It was decided, wisely I believe, that "Solitary Man" would be the first release under Diamond's new deal.

"Solitary Man" is a song that would forever add a certain gravity to Diamond's emerging persona. Its depiction of a kind of brooding, romantic isolation was extremely convincing—even, as it turned out, to Diamond himself.

When discussing "Solitary Man," Neil noted that the song, written in the new home in Massapequa he shared with Jaye, "convinced me I'd always been this quiet, introverted kid." He then confessed that a schoolmate recently came backstage and showed him their sixth-grade graduation book. "I was shocked to be reminded that I had been voted 'Most Cheerful.'" That totally shook my whole concept of what I was like as a child. I thought I was a loner and it turns out I was probably a cheerleader." Of course, as Diamond went on to point out, a song called "Cheerful Man" would not have had quite the same ring to it.

Before his new label could release "Solitary Man" (or even "Cheerful Man") Diamond quite nearly changed his whole identity and made perhaps the single goofiest and most misbegotten career decision of his entire life. And though I have challenged him every time he's told me the story, Diamond has long insisted that he actually considered changing his stage name from his real name, Neil Diamond, to—of all things—Eice Cherry or Noah Kaminsky.

"While the label was writing a new biography, I thought maybe I should have a different name," he said, explaining that at that point in music history, it seemed extremely unclear how long this whole rock and roll world would last. And while he knew he would always be a songwriter, he couldn't even imagine at that point that his lifespan as a recording artist would be all that long. "This was all going to be some kind of giggle that I'd be able to show my grandchildren," the once and future Diamond explained. "So I flirted with using a pseudonym. But needless to say, I'm very relieved that I didn't."

Neil told me that when it came right down to it, he just couldn't figure out how to explain changing his name to his grandmother, suggesting perhaps that one should really never do *anything* that can't be fully justified to a grandparent.

With the gift of retrospection, Eice Cherry now seems silly enough, even if Diamond's sweet next single, "Cherry, Cherry," was already waiting in the wings. But did a bright fellow lucky enough to be born as Neil Diamond really think that he was going to make it big instead as Noah Kaminsky?

"Yeah, of course," Diamond told me with a laugh. "I mean, if Simon and *Garfunkel* could do it, Noah Kaminsky could do it."

By any name and any standard, Neil Diamond's life was about to get a lot less solitary.

CHERRY, CHERRY AND TWENTY-FOUR OTHER WAYS TO MOVE ME

Do it
While your soul's still burnin'
You know I'll be yearnin' away
Say what you want to say

—"DO IT," BY NEIL DIAMOND

EVERYBODY LOVES SOME KIND OF MUSIC, SOMETIME. IN MY LIFE, I have found this to be true with everybody I've ever met from presidents to punks, with the possible exception of Paris Hilton, who, when I once questioned her on the subject, could not tell me *any* music she thought was hot.

Once while working writing a White House TV special, I was standing in a big tent on the South Lawn when President Clinton chose to leave the Oval Office during some minor international crisis to join the show's production team in checking out the rehearsals of Al

Green and John Fogerty. While some foreign affairs hard-liners might find this decision questionable, to any true music lover this is obviously the kind of wise judgment that we so sorely need in the leader of the free world.

My own favorite music of all time tends to come in what Elton John once described to me as "purple patches"—specific time periods when great artists fall into an extended groove and release much of their finest work in a concentrated blast of pure artistic excellence.

To name just a few of my favorite things, my most prized purple patches include Frank Sinatra's work on Capitol, then Reprise Records; Ray Charles' entire tenure on Atlantic Records; the Beatles during *Rubber Soul* and *Revolver*; every single note Bob Dylan recorded in the sixties and again as a gospel artist in the late seventies and early eighties; the early Who; Elvis Presley's surprise late-sixties Memphis comeback; Sly and the Family Stone from *Stand!* to *Fresh*; the Rolling Stones from *Let It Bleed* to *Black & Blue*; Stevie Wonder's run from *Talking Book* to *Songs in the Key of Life*; Elton John from *Tumbleweed Connection* to *Goodbye Yellow Brick Road*; Al Green's entire time on Hi Records; Carole King for a few years before and after *Tapestry*; the Atlantic recordings of Daryl Hall & John Oates, especially *Abandoned Luncheonette*; Bruce Springsteen from *The Wild, the Innocent and the E Street Shuffle* through *The River* and then again on *Tunnel of Love*; Elvis Costello and the Attractions from *This Year's Model* through *Armed Forces*; Tom Petty & the Heartbreakers from *Damn the Torpedos* through *Long After Dark*, and again after *Wildflowers*; Prince from *Dirty Mind* to *Sign of the Times*; the Clash on *London Calling* and stray parts of *Sandinista*; the Replacements from *Let It Be* to *All Shook Down;* and Nirvana from *Nevermind* right until Kurt Cobain's premature finale.

Finally—as much as anything else in the whole wide world, apart from my own wife and kids—I shall forever love, honor, and obey the timeless music that we are about to celebrate together. So let us all now praise some famous songs, the ones by which a wide world of fans would first discover *The Feel of Neil Diamond.*

Ladies and gentlemen, and anybody else who might be out there reading these words, all hail the 1965–1968 Bang recordings of Mr. Neil Diamond.

Now *that's* hot.

For seven long years, Neil Diamond had been busy beating down doors all around New York City's Tin Pan Alley, trying everything that he could think of to make some beautiful noise as a struggling singer-songwriter. Considering the tremendous talent that Diamond would so very soon demonstrate, he did so with remarkably little success. Now at the age of twenty-four, Diamond was already a man faced with some serious responsibilities and the prospects that his dream might never come true. "There was the pressure of being a dad, being a husband, I couldn't just fool around," Neil says. "I had to get down to business and *really* make it."

As the second half of the sixties got under way, things started turning around for Diamond in a very big way. After the better part of a decade full of near misses and outright rejection, Diamond finally started to really make it, and suddenly he had plenty happening on numerous musical fronts in 1965. Thankfully, the most happening thing of all was the remarkable and frequently exquisite new music that he found himself making with his new mentors, partners, and friends, Jeff Barry and Ellie Greenwich.

Call it pop. Call it rock. Call it existential bubblegum.

By any name, the twenty-five master recordings that Neil Diamond cut for Bang Records between 1965 and 1968 are genuinely extraordinary. From "Solitary Man" to "Cherry, Cherry" to "Girl, You'll

Be a Woman Soon" to "Thank the Lord for the Night Time" to "Shilo," the Bang recordings remain among Diamond's most sparkling gems. The Bang Records logo was a simple comic book–style drawing of a gun, and fittingly, the songs that Bang brought to the world would at long last bullet Diamond straight to the top.

One need not formulate a big Bang theory to comprehend why Neil Diamond so quickly exploded at his new label. The record—and the records—shows that the Bang recordings presented the perfect marriage of Jeff Barry and Ellie Greenwich's unabashed pop smarts and proven craftsmanship as hit makers with Neil's far more raw and confessional approach. Though Barry and Greenwich were already falling apart as a married couple by now, these talented collaborators nonetheless came together beautifully to give Diamond his invaluable graduate degree on how to make memorable and commercial music. They brought the best of the Brill Building instincts; Diamond brought the shock of the new that would lead the way towards the whole new introspective singer-songwriter movement.

The happy results of this mutually beneficial musical partnership came now in a series of unforgettable three-chord operas, to borrow a memorable phrase that Diamond would use as an album title many years later. There were also a few other all-stars on the winning team creating this body of work, notably two great engineers who went on to become future distinguished record producers in their own right—Phil Ramone and Brooks Arthur—as well as the exceptionally gifted arranger Artie Butler.

For all the team offered, Diamond brought a great deal to this particular musical party. Neil's increasingly unique material and delivery brought Barry and Greenwich and their studio A-team something very special: material of growing depth and gravity that successfully conveyed emotions considerably more adult and weighty than ones they had come to expect from the girl groups and boy singers of the early sixties.

Lest we forget, the second word in "Solitary Man" is "Man," and I would argue it was Diamond's grown-up masculinity and transparent brooding intensity that would allow Barry and Greenwich's sublimely constructed recordings to transform him into a real, iconic star. Just as groundbreaking and game-changing artists like Bob Dylan and the Beatles were bringing a new energy and a new sense of possibility to the world's popular music in this era, Diamond now began fully investing his own natural sense of drama into the vital new songs that he was writing. After years of flailing around professionally with little luck to write hit songs for others, Neil Diamond was beginning to find his own voice. In a 1976 profile in *Rolling Stone* by Ben Fong Torres, one of my favorite music writers, Diamond provided a hint as to the roots of this newfound intensity. "It's very difficult to accept seven years of failing without it doing something to you," Diamond admitted. "And what it did was close me up as a person."

If Diamond's long haul to the top indeed closed him up on some personal level, it also seems to have caused him to throw more and more of himself into his music. In Neil's suddenly more deeply felt, introspective music, one could feel not simply the desire to have a hit but, more seductively, a growing passion to be understood on some primal, psychological level. As John Lennon was doing with the Beatles in a song like "I'm a Loser," Diamond started using the popular song as a more open sort of forum for personal exploration and revelation. In retrospect, a song like "Solitary Man," recorded in 1965, now stands as an early example of the sort of confessional, even therapeutic writing that would flower in the decade to come. More and more, Diamond was making music with a genuine sense of purpose.

Of the twenty-five tracks recorded for the Bang label, nearly half can still be heard today on an album that is quite rightly called *Classics*. The collection's subtitle would declare these to be *Early Songs*, but in truth these are the sorts of evergreen popular recordings that never grow dated. In the liner notes to the *In My Lifetime* box set, I demonstrated my usual flair for understatement when I described the Bang recordings as "the Dead Sea Scrolls or Rosetta Stones of the Diamond oeuvre."

For all that grand praise, however, it is the immediacy and the relatively spare sound of the tracks that helped make them so undeniable even forty years later. "There was definitely a simplicity to the Bang songs," Diamond says, "because I didn't have anything to live up to. I didn't have a year to ponder a lyric." Sometimes, as Leonardo da Vinci once put it, "simplicity is the ultimate sophistication."

A masterpiece full of musical and lyrical mystique, "Solitary Man" benefited enormously from the addition of trombones on the chorus, the sort of musical punctuation point from Barry and Greenwich that somehow made all the difference. When "Solitary Man" was released as Diamond's first single for his new label, an ad in *Billboard* declared, "Bang Records proudly announces the birth of a great new artist, Neil Diamond." For once, you could actually believe the hype.

Though "Solitary Man," with the inspiring and inspired song "Do It" on the flip side, backed up Bang's bold claim and then some, this future pop standard initially cracked the top ten in just a few major radio markets, peaking at only #55 on the national *Billboard* charts. For such a breakthrough recording, this moderate commercial success now seems extremely disappointing. Fortunately, Bang's founder, Bert Berns, was an astute enough music man to know full well that Diamond had lots more to offer. And fortunately, Berns and company wouldn't have to keep the faith very long, as it was Diamond's even more infectious next single that would ultimately seal the deal and at last make him a full-blown star.

"Cherry, Cherry," arguably the single most undeniable pop-rocker in the entire Diamond cannon, began its long, productive life when Neil, Jeff Barry, and Ellie Greenwich were hanging around a small office at Bang Records discussing material for his first session for the label. "I began to play a guitar lick which caught Jeff's ear," Diamond told me once. "His positive reaction made me go home and finish 'Cherry, Cherry.'" Interestingly, years later Jeff Barry would give an interview in England's *Melody Maker* in which he suggested that the song was originally written as "Money, Money," but that he and Bert Berns convinced Diamond it would be wise to go with a title that was more teen friendly and fun. (None of this would stop Tommy James & the Shondells, who had enjoyed a huge hit with Barry and Greenwich's "Hanky Panky" in 1965, from later having a smash with "Mony, Mony," a profitably "Cherry, Cherry"-adjacent-sounding pop smash in 1968.)

To record "Cherry, Cherry," the trio went into Dick Charles' studio in New York and recorded a stripped-down demo version of this catchy new number that featured Diamond playing guitar and singing the poppy yet sexy lead vocal. Barry and Greenwich contributed the vocal background parts with their usual grace and gusto. Session great Artie Butler added piano and Hammond organ. "I forget who played bass, but bless him anyway," Diamond recalled in the liner notes of *In My Lifetime.* Beyond those basics, they then added some extremely convincing hand claps and a few other little rhythmic touches but no actual drums to this demo.

Following the standard routine, the same winning team then assembled to go about making a significantly more produced official recording of "Cherry, Cherry," one complete with horns and drums. Although Diamond would say this bigger and more produced version of the song—made available decades later on the *In My Lifetime* anthology—had its own energy, they all decided that it was ultimately lacking "the simplicity and groove of the demo," as Diamond put it. Following their instincts, the demo version was instead released as Diamond's second single for Bang. Even without drums or the usual polish, this demo version of "Cherry, Cherry" was a smash, going all the way to #6 in America and even helping to spread the name and sound of Neil Diamond around the world. As Neil would note with nice understatement in his comments on *In My Lifetime*, "I think we made the right choice."

Indeed, they had.

Suddenly, as in a long dreamed of but long denied flash, Neil Diamond had now gone from "Who's Neil Diamond?" to "Get me some of that Neil Diamond!" In the preceding months, as if sensing something happening in the air, a number of recording acts both here and abroad had begun to cut some of the tunes Diamond had been writing. For example, a group called the Solitaires recorded one song called "Fool That I Am." Jan Tanzy cut "That New Boy in Town," a number Diamond had written with his friend Carl D'Errico. British superstar Cliff Richard cut "Just Another Guy," while America pop favorite Bobby Vinton recorded "Don't Go Away Mad." None of these covers of Diamond compositions were major hits, yet with the sudden success of Diamond's own recording of "Cherry, Cherry," his stock as a songwriter for hire was rising as well.

Brill Building powerhouse Don Kirshner, who was looking for hit material for America's answer to the Beatles, the new TV sensations the Monkees, loved "Cherry, Cherry" just as anyone with functioning ears would. Kirshner asked Jeff Barry if Diamond might have anything else suitable for his now red hot TV group. "Jeff and I went over to see Don," Neil recalled to me in the notes for *In My Lifetime*. "I knew I was making it because it was the first time I had ever been invited into this kingmaker's office." Kirshner responded favorably to "I'm a Believer" immediately, and after assuring Neil that he could publish the song too, Diamond's Monkees business could begin.

In 1966, the often underrated Pre-Fab Four's rendition of "I'm a Believer," featuring a convincing lead vocal by Mickey Dolenz, went to #1 for seven straight weeks, becoming the single biggest hit in what was a remarkable musical year. In 1967, another Diamond composition, "A Little Bit Me, a Little Bit You," would *merely* go to #2. After years of feeling as if he could get nothing quite right, Diamond must have suddenly felt as if he could hardly do anything wrong.

Yet it was Diamond's own recordings of the era that are ultimately the most impressive. With considerable help from Barry and Greenwich, Diamond's learning curve was wildly impressive, as each new song he released seemed to expand his range and deepen the impression that his obvious talent was making.

Diamond's first ever album, called *The Feel of Neil Diamond,* was pushed out to capitalize on the success of "Cherry, Cherry." Bert Berns contributed liner notes that suggest why. "The phones in our offices are ringing like mad," he wrote. "Distributors all over the country are screaming for a Neil Diamond LP." Despite many great moments, *The Feel of Neil Diamond* felt in some ways like a rush job, particularly because of its reliance on a number of covers of recent hits, including a version of Barry and Greenwich's "Hanky Panky," which Neil audibly and playfully resisted singing. In retrospect, perhaps he should have resisted singing "La Bamba" too.

On the other hand, Diamond did much better with his rendition of the Cyrkle folk-rock charmer "Red Rubber Ball" and a faithful but pleasant version of the Mamas and the Papas' smash "Monday, Monday." Still, somehow, despite including "Solitary Man," "Cherry, Cherry," and his newest hit "I Got the Feelin' (Oh, No, No)," *The Feel of Neil Diamond* would not break the top forty on the album charts. In fact, it even missed out cracking the top one hundred and forty by *that* much. This chart placement would be Diamond's first reason to believe that the more singles-driven Bang label might not be big enough, or album-oriented enough, for his growing ambition.

Still, with each new single, Diamond's range seemed to expand as the depth of his talent became more obvious and widely appreciated.

Diamond has described "I Got the Feelin' (Oh, No, No)," which went to #16 on the *Billboard* singles chart, as being "my first attempt to extend the emotional and stylistic range of my voice. The song was pretty basic, but it was a conscious effort to expand my vocal horizons and connect with the song as a singer." A brooding song of romantic disharmony, "I Got the Feelin' (Oh No, No)" built from a folkish start to a big conclusion, all in two minutes and thirteen seconds. Bang followed with "You Got to Me"—a winning and sexy rocker propelled by some mean harmonica-playing up front, and some more of Barry and Greenwich's excellent call-and-response backing vocals—that also took its place in the top twenty, hitting #18.

Next came one of Diamond's eternal-young-ladies choice numbers, "Girl, You'll Be a Woman Soon," the song that would eventually get a whole new high life in the nineties, thanks to Quentin Tarantino's *Pulp Fiction*. When Diamond first recorded the slow, seductively sensitive song in 1967, it solidified his growing connection with his young female fan base, many of whom are apparently still following him all these years later, even if they are no longer properly addressed as "girl." Diamond has said that the song was written for all those teenaged girls who would show up at his earliest tour dates and vocally express their tremendous support. "All those ooohs and ahhhs and screams made me laugh a little," Diamond recalled. "It threw me for a loop at first and then I decided to write a song with these girls in mind." Apparently all those young ladies appreciated the kind gesture, rewarding Diamond with his second top-ten hit as a recording artist.

In the summer of 1967, Bang released "Thank the Lord for the Night Time" around the same time that it put out Diamond's second long-player titled *Just for You*. "Thank the Lord for the Night Time," which hit #13 on the charts, was another song that helped shape Diamond's persona with its ingenious and compelling and apparently appealing blend of gospel spirit and brooding romance. "A rock & roll song with some black music influence" is how Diamond described it for *In My Lifetime*. "I've always been moved by gospel music and 'Thank the Lord for the Night Time' is probably as close as this white Jewish kid from Brooklyn could come to being a gospel singer."

The new *Just for You* album featured a few of Diamond's past hits like "Solitary Man," "Cherry, Cherry" (both already on *The Feel of Neil Diamond*) as well as "You Got to Me" and "The Boat That I Row," which had originally been released as the B side of "I Got the Feelin' (Oh No, No)." In 1996, Diamond said that he considered "The Boat That I Row" to be "my first rebel song," calling it one of his first compositions "reflecting my growing independence. This is the way I am, my boat is tiny and the direction it takes may not follow the standard routes, but if you like what you see, come on along and join me on this journey." The British singer Lulu of "To Sir with Love" fame would also record "The Boat That I Row," but there could be no doubt about who was ultimately rowing this boat.

Just for You also included one of the undervalued, little heard lost gems of Diamond's early recording years, a catchy midtempo pop rock winner called "The Long Way Home" that was easily Diamond's most Beatlesque effort yet.

In the end, *Just for You* would do better on the charts than *The Feel of Neil Diamond*, but for all of his recent success on the singles charts, Diamond's second album still only hit a relatively disappointing #80. Coming in the same revolutionary year of *Sgt. Pepper's Lonely Hearts Club Band*, when the rock album was officially becoming a respected and fashionable art form, such a chart performance must have been discouraging for Diamond.

Finally, though, it was not simply this weak performance in the album market that would bring a great and productive era in Diamond's career to a sudden conclusion. In the end, it was a more personal slight related to another gem of a song on *Just for You* that would motivate Diamond to make another big move in his career.

Rather than release Diamond's choice for his next single, "Shilo," Berns insisted on releasing a new song that was inspired by Diamond's sudden rush of road trips to promote his hits. "Kentucky Woman" was a strong country-tinged number that Diamond had written while on his first real tour as part of a thirty-two-city, twenty-eight-day run of dates with the Dick Clark Caravan, which found him sharing a bill with Tommy Roe, Billy Joe Royal, and P. J. Proby. "We attracted teenage girls almost exclusively and the house, usually a high school auditorium, was filled to the rafters with screaming females night after night," Diamond recalled on *In My Lifetime*. "Kentucky Woman" he remembered as being written in the back of a limo he had bought for $1,500 "as we approached the outskirts of Paducah, Kentucky"—an excellent song, not to mention a spectacular price for a limo.

With hits on the radio, Diamond found himself taking his act on the road with increasing frequency, sharing the stage with boy singers and louder acts like Vanilla Fudge alike. Some of these bills made more sense than others. Once Diamond found himself serving as the unlikely middleman between Herman's Hermits and the Who. As Diamond described it, this would prove to be a night to remember. "The closing act was the Who—who I never heard of," he confessed. "And they got out there and started smashing up their amps, and equipment and guitars. I have *never* smashed a guitar. I leave that to other people. I like my guitars."

Finally, though, it was the decision as to what song would follow "Thank the Lord for the Night Time" that would derail Diamond's musical journey with Bang. While he liked "Kentucky Woman" too, Diamond was feeling justifiably excited about the new song he had written called "Shilo" that appeared to draw on vivid child memories of inner lives and imaginary friends. In his song-by-song comments for *In My Lifetime*, Diamond described "Shilo" as "my first attempt at creating a fantasy life—in a song, that is." He went on to correctly identify "Shilo" as "the song that ended my relationship with Bang Records, who did not see this as 'in the Neil Diamond hit mode' (whatever that might be)." Diamond would point out that the song, while never a chart smash, has remained a treasured audience favorite over the years. As he put it, "Maybe the audience senses that it really is me talking."

Still, following his own proven commercial instincts, Berns balked at releasing "Shilo" as a single, favoring instead "Kentucky Woman," which climbed as high as #22. For the time being, "Shilo" was consigned to being merely an album track on *Just for You*.

Unfortunately for him, Bert Berns' decision not to fully support Diamond's desire to stretch himself artistically would cost Bang dearly. Now openly frustrated with his current recording situation, Diamond and his legal advisors started what would become the process of leaving Bang behind, ending his very close professional relationship with Jeff Barry and Ellie Greenwich on a sadly unpleasant note.

Things would get considerably worse between Diamond and Bert Berns once Diamond made it clear that he was done recording for

Bang. By all accounts, Berns was a great music man and an interesting and colorful character. In a 1998 piece in the British music magazine *Mojo*, writer Barney Hoskyns quoted Jerry Wexler as describing
Berns as "a paunchy, nervous cat with a shock of unruly black hair."
Wexler went on to add, "He liked the company of gangsters, and he
boasted that he'd run guns and dope in Havana of the 1950s."

Certainly Berns was wise when it came to making music as well as
when it came to making money while making music. Berns' favored
sound was a sort of symphonic soul, and he made great records for the
likes of Solomon Burke and Ben E. King. He cowrote "Piece of My
Heart" with Jerry Ragovoy. He wrote and produced "Twist and Shout"
for the Isley Brothers. He took over the Drifters from Lieber and
Stoller. In recent years, I asked Van Morrison about Berns, who had
produced "Brown Eyed Girl," after all, and his immediate reaction was
revealing. Musically, Morrison told me, Berns was a great mentor and
genuine major talent. In terms of business, Morrison suggested, his
relatively short time with Berns had been educational in a less pleasant
manner.

There can be little doubt that Bert Berns understood what he was
losing with Neil Diamond's departure. In the notes to a 2002 anthology of Berns' work, his son Brett quoted his father as writing of Diamond that "every generation yields one truly great individual who
stands out among all others due to style, originality, creativeness, sus-
taining power, and genius."

Losing a genius, particularly such a profitable one, would be a
major blow to any label, especially a young and small company like
Bang. Over the years, the generally diplomatic Diamond has spoken
about the intense pressure that he felt in the wake of his decision to
strike out on his own and leave Bang Records. During his 1976 interview with Ben Fong Torres in *Rolling Stone*, Diamond recalled that

when he informed Berns that he would not record for him anymore, "the heat began to get really intense."

Stories have repeatedly surfaced that some sort of bomb, most likely a smoke bomb, was thrown into the Bitter End, the New York City nightclub owned by Diamond's then manager, Fred Weintraub. Even more recently, as late as 2002, Diamond was quoted as telling the *London Standard*, "I carried a .38 for six months after I left Bang Records in 1968. I had a warning from the FBI to protect myself. So I sent my family away and started carrying a gun. Was I scared? I was scared 24/7."

Sadly, the notion that Diamond was being intimidated in retaliation for leaving Bang would be completely denied not by Berns, but rather by his widow, Ilene Berns. As fate would have it, Bert Berns himself would die on December 31, 1967, at age thirty-five, of heart failure.

In leaving Bang Records, Neil Diamond proved once again that he would do whatever it took to continue to grow as an artist and get his share of control in art, in business, and in life.

By 1967, it was clear that Diamond was torn between his own desire to go further as an artist and his label's predictable desire to keep the gravy train on the tracks. Even when he had to appear in a relatively lightweight publication like *Hit Parader*, Diamond found a way to do so on his own less than frivolous terms. In one article that he wrote (or had ghostwritten) Diamond spoke with considerable seriousness about his own artistic approach to the music he was making: "There are young writers who can compare with any of the great writers of the past. That's why I always laugh when people put down rock & roll . . . There are people writing in the rock idiom now who will be here twenty years from now writing good music. It's a very exciting time."

Diamond made a similar point in a *Billboard* profile of him that same year. "If a writer takes himself seriously," he noted, "he will constantly experiment with not necessarily avant-garde material but with relatively untried musical and lyrical material."

Read between any of those lines, and you can tell that Neil Diamond was much more interested in being one of those serious writers than in being the last man left in the Brill Building trying to rewrite "Cherry, Cherry" over and over again until it lost any flavor.

"They began to want and expect music that I had already done," Diamond said. "They wanted more 'Cherry Cherry' and 'Kentucky Woman' and 'Solitary Man' and I had gone past that."

Diamond had always respected the great writers of the Brill Building era. Yet at the same time he was intuitive enough to sense that the times really were changing now, and changing *fast*. When I asked him in 1988 what had been lost when the Brill Building era ended, Neil answered, "Well, I would have loved to have heard another ten years of creative, successful music from the writers of that time. But I'm not so sure if I would trade it for what was to come." Given the choice, Diamond took another big risk to become part of whatever braver, newer musical world was brewing.

Neil Diamond had entered 1965 a total unknown. By 1967, a poll of DJs in the music industry trade publication *Cash Box* identified him as the "most promising up and coming male vocalist." By the end of this same year, the same publication declared in a separate survey that Diamond was tied for the honor of being America's number-one singer of 1967. That other singer's name was Frank Sinatra.

Clearly, Diamond was a significant star on the rise, yet not for the last time, he still found himself feeling like the odd solitary man out. In 1988, asked if he felt like part of the rock scene when he had those early first hits for Bang Records, his answer was emphatic. He spoke of the isolation of being a single artist at a time when groups were ruling the world. "People didn't know exactly what to make of me," he told me. "There's the LSD scene in San Francisco, and there's the folk scene in New York. There's all kinds of English music coming over, and here comes a guy with a guitar, and I didn't really fit into what was happening in music."

Diamond went on to explain that he felt as if the critics of the day had no time for him. "I did a show at Carnegie Hall as a way to showcase myself," he remembered. "No reviewers showed up. People weren't looking to some guy with a guitar who, while nobody was looking, had ten hit records in a row. It was like I didn't exist."

Soon the whole world would know that Neil Diamond did exist, but as the sixties ended, his continuing pursuit of a dream now coming true would cost him both his home and his first marriage.

A SONG SUNG BLUE
ON GLORY ROAD

Home is a wounded heart

Haven't you heard the story?

He's out for love and for glory

And she's waitin' home by the fire

—"HOME IS A WOUNDED HEART," BY NEIL DIAMOND

IN THE WONDERFULLY EMOTIONAL AND OCCASIONALLY MANIC-depressive world of Neil Diamond, agony and ecstasy have long gone hand in hand, making no shortage of beautiful music together. This sweet-and-sour duality seems like an accurate reflection of the sort of blessed yet complex life that Diamond, like many of us, has led. For instance, in the high-scoring, action-packed second half of the 1960s, just as Diamond's career was finally taking off, his first marriage was falling apart. This turn of events must have felt all the more devastating for the Diamond family, since the couple already had one young daughter with another on the way.

Over the years, Diamond has repeatedly taken the blame for the failure of his first marriage, citing his zealous dedication to his career as the only real mitigating factor. "You jump on this wild horse and you're just holding on for dear life," Neil said. "I think it was responsible in a large way for ending my first marriage. And it was painful."

As a surviving yet whining child of divorce myself, I can report firsthand that Neil Sedaka really knew what he was singing about—breaking up *is* hard to do. Divorce was becoming all the rage when Diamond's first marriage ended, one of the logical but nonetheless profoundly hurtful side effects of a larger cultural tendency toward doing one's own thing. Diamond suggested as much in his 1976 *Rolling Stone* interview with Ben Fong-Torres:

"It was almost as though our destiny was preordained," Diamond said. "We were to be married, have children; the best we could hope for was a little house on Long Island. We'd live the lives our parents wanted us to live. I didn't really begin to think about myself and my life until I began to travel and remove myself from that peer group. And I realized that that wasn't what I wanted at all, and things began to deteriorate from that point. I just decided to split and leave it all behind. In a sense it was running away."

Like everything else in Diamond's life, such personal trauma would eventually find its way into his music, sometimes masked, sometimes more obvious. If a song like "Solitary Man" was a young man's romantic declaration of independence, Diamond was now gaining the sort of grown-up experience in real life that would inform his songs forever more. Love, both lost and found, remains one of the central and eternal themes for most songwriters worthy of the title, and for Diamond more than most.

As a rule, the more lived-in the song feels, the deeper it cuts. A Diamond song from the late sixties called "Hurting You Don't Come Easy" would seem to be one reflection of both the man's sense of guilt and his determination to move on. For my money, his most powerful statement on this subject came years later when he perhaps had more perspective. Right around the time that my own parents were going through their own marital battle royal in the New Jersey courts during our bicentennial year, Diamond would release a powerful ballad on his highly autobiographical *Beautiful Noise* album called "Home Is a Wounded Heart." At the time, I only knew it touched me. Today it is hard for me not to hear it as the man's extremely moving acknowledgment of the pain that he inflicted in his first marriage:

> *Home is a wounded heart*
> *haven't you heard the story?*
> *He's out for love and for glory*
> *and she's waitin' home by the fire*
>
> *And wasn't it yesterday*
> *wasn't it me who said it?*
> *I swore that you'd never regret it*
> *Now home is a wounded heart*

In all the times that I have ever spoken with Neil Diamond over the years, on or off the record, I have never heard him say a bad word about either of the two women he married, or really anyone else for that matter. Other than self-deprecation, which he engages in with considerable ease and skill, Diamond tends to keep things very positive, at least in the presence of a friendly member of the media. And whether out of guilt, gallantry, or perhaps a canny sense of the psychology of his predominantly female fan base, Diamond has frequently praised the women in his life, past and present.

In 1994, for a piece in *Interview* magazine, Diamond had an interesting conversation with Carole Bayer Sager, another former Brill Building denizen with whom he would collaborate successfully in the eighties, along with her then husband Burt Bacharach. Sager asked Diamond, then married to his second wife, Marcia, for a quarter century, if he could go back over his life and change only one thing, what it would be.

After pausing, Diamond told Sager, "I might not have gotten divorced so fast the first time. I gave up on my first marriage without knowing what I was giving up. Not that for a moment I would change what the last twenty-five years have brought for me, because I'm married to the right woman."

That right woman of whom Diamond spoke so fondly was the former Marcia Murphey, who in 1969 became Diamond's second wife. He first met the attractive, blond Murphey while she was working as a production assistant on a New York TV dance program called *The Clay Cole Show*. Diamond has suggested that he was drawn to Murphey immediately, often citing a certain sadness in her eyes that caught his attention. Yet by all accounts, Diamond and Murphey were immediately very happy together, a happiness that could soon be heard coming through loud and clear in some of the new songs that Diamond was writing, like "Practically Newborn," a buoyant number about love's ability to "take me out of my doubt and fears," leaving him, in essence, reborn.

In a sense, Neil Diamond was born again at the end of the sixties, and that rebirth meant leaving much behind him. On the personal front, Diamond left his wife, putting a painful distance between himself and his two young daughters. In his professional life, Diamond left behind not only Bang Records, but also before very long his manager, Fred Weintraub, and the very city that had helped shape him and his music. Diamond followed his muse and his music, as he would time and time again, moving to Los Angeles as part of a new start.

After obtaining his legal freedom from Bang in the spring of 1968, Diamond was now free to sign a new deal with MCA's small Uni label, which he did, in April. Diamond would get a $250,000 guarantee for eight albums, an extremely lucrative deal at the time, and one that he believed would give him better promotion and newfound artistic freedom. In 1968, not wasting any time, he called together a session with a new team of producers: singer-songwriter Chip Taylor (who wrote "Wild Thing" and is also the brother of actor of Jon Voight) and Al Gorgoni (a session guitar great). Together they recorded one single. The B side recorded with Diamond's touring band was called "Holiday Inn Blues" and captured the essence of life on the road in its opening lines: "Half a day from nowhere / Hurrying to get there." The A side was concerned not with where Diamond was going, but where he came from, and the result was quite possibly the single most affecting song of Diamond's entire career, "Brooklyn Roads."

"Brooklyn Roads," with its vivid evocation of childhood, was initially not the smash hit it deserved to be. Part of the problem was that Bang Records did not let go of Diamond easily. Indeed, the market was flooded with a procession of releases and rereleases that seemed designed to confuse the consumer as well as squeeze every last dime to be had out of his twenty-five recordings. Ironically, around the same time that the deeply personal "Brooklyn Roads" was released by Diamond's new label, his old friends at Bang saw fit to release "Shilo" as a single, just as he had once begged them to do. Now effectively competing with himself, Diamond must have had mixed feelings as "Shilo" rose to #24 on the *Billboard* charts, while "Brooklyn Roads" stopped at #55. "I had just signed with MCA Records and wanted to stretch my creative wings," Diamond said. Calling this "the most literal and personal story I had written up to that point," he noted that he "loved the freedom of being able to write something without the charts in mind."

Remarkably, this cat-and-mouse game of overlapping releases would continue for years, as Bang found new and arguably creative ways to repurpose Neil's old tracks into a series of new singles and albums. While actually at the label, Diamond had released only two albums, *The Feel of Neil Diamond* and *Just for You*. After he left the label, suddenly record store racks were stuffed with a series of "new" album releases with titles like *Neil Diamond's Greatest Hits*, *Shilo*, *Do It*, the cassette-only release of *The Very Best of Neil Diamond*, and *Double Gold*. Let it never be said that the folks at Bang didn't believe in recycling.

Thanks to the strength of Diamond's back catalog, Bang also enjoyed success on the singles chart with "New Orleans" (#55), "Red, Red Wine" (#62), a rereleased "Solitary Man" (#21, far better than the song did the first time around), "Do It" (the original flip side of "Solitary Man" now rising to #36 on its own strength), Diamond's version of "I'm a Believer" (#51), and "The Long Way Home (#91). This seemingly unending procession of releases served to greatly muddy the waters for Diamond's actual brand new recordings for the Uni label. It also helps explain why Diamond would ultimately buy back his Bang masters himself, so as to control his own work in the future. So if Bang Records wanted to teach Neil Diamond a lesson with all these reissues, in the end they did exactly that—and a very profitable lesson for Diamond as it would turn out.

Diamond's first album for Uni would be released under the unusual title *Velvet Gloves and Spit*, and it is an unusual album of tremendous high points and at least one truly jaw-dropping if entirely fascinating low point. Beyond both sides of the "Brooklyn Roads" and "Holiday Inn Blues" single, the highlights here included "Two-Bit Manchild," a fantastically rhythmic sort of hymn to hedonism that only climbed to #66 on the *Billboard* charts, two spots better than another of the singles from the album, the sunny if slight "Sunday Sun," and "Practically Newborn," which sounds like a personal and blissful celebration of romantic love, entirely stiffed on the charts. All three of these new songs were ably produced by Tom Catalano. Catalano, the same man who had helped Diamond get his first, short-lived single deal at Columbia in the early sixties, now reemerged in Diamond's career as one of his chief collaborators in the years to come.

Things got decidedly stranger on *Velvet Gloves and Spit* with a novelty number entitled "Knackelflerg" that sounds like some demented parody of a sixties movie theme. Embarrassingly, I have never asked Neil about "Knackelflerg," mostly because doing so would have meant trying to pronounce it, and frankly that seemed like more trouble than it was worth. Forty years later, "Knackelflerg" remains a compelling, cabaret-sounding head-scratcher. Yet somehow, a song called "Knackelflerg" was emphatically not the strangest song on the album.

Absolutely nothing in the entire Neil Diamond canon—or for that matter, in life itself—could ever possibly prepare one for *Velvet Gloves and Spit*'s mad and misconceived big statement. "The Pot Smoker's Song" is an antidrug protest song so profoundly messed up that one can in a way only hope that someone involved in its creation was, paradoxically speaking, very, *very* high. In the end, Diamond's debut for his new label was perhaps a little too all over the place for its own good. It was as if now, finally having earned the freedom to do anything, Neil Diamond was desperately rushing to do *everything*.

Having come into the MCA fold in hopes of becoming much more of an album artist, it had to be worrying that *Velvet Gloves and Spit* completely failed to break into the *Billboard* top two hundred, a worse performance than either of Diamond's first two albums at Bang. Instead of taking that next giant step forward, Diamond found himself losing ground.

Looking to make another change, Diamond headed down to American Sound Studios in Memphis, Tennessee, a famously funky spot in a rundown section in the north part of town. By January 1969, the music universe was becoming far less centered in New York, and

American Sound was on a hot streak, churning out soulful but pop-radio-friendly tracks like "The Letter" by the Box Tops and "Son of a Preacher Man" by Dusty Springfield, among many other more straight-ahead soul hits for Wilson Pickett and Joe Tex. As if to indicate the buzz on the place, Diamond was scheduled to come into American Sound Studios just ahead of the recently revitalized Elvis Presley, who was then still hot off his *Elvis* comeback TV special.

It is with great spiritual pride that I tell you our Jewish Elvis was quick enough to beat that *other* Elvis to the punch here, though Diamond's schedule would be moved around a bit to accommodate the pressing needs of the King. Perhaps this regal competition for studio space at American Sound helps explain why Diamond wasted no time with his first session there. Diamond would be working with producer and owner Chips Moman, producer and bass player Tommy Cogbill, as well as a group of first-call session musicians for whom American Sound was becoming a musical home: keyboard players Bobby Emmons and Bobby Wood, guitarist Reggie Young, drummer Gene Christman, and Mike Leech, who played bass when Cogbill was busy producing.

As Diamond once told me, he wrote the lyrics to "Brother Love's Traveling Salvation Show" on his flight south to Memphis, setting new words to a rousing, soulful tune that he already had. These new lyrics, a sort of *Elmer Gantry*–inspired morality tale juxtaposed with one Brooklyn kid's version of Southern soul, was a major breakthrough moment for Diamond.

"Brother Love's Traveling Salvation Show" would give Diamond a flesh-and-blood, morally ambiguous character to play: a charismatic preacher working a crowd. Becoming "Brother Love," at least for three and a half minutes, took Diamond further outside of himself in a very powerful way. "The story of 'Brother Love' demanded its own place in those sessions and was recorded the following day with nary a change in the lyrics," Diamond recalled in the liner notes of *In My Lifetime*. "This recording became a hit and was to make a showman out of me. How could you *not* let go of your inhibitions when playing such a wonderful character?"

If Diamond had been struggling to truly move past his Bang recordings, he won that struggle with the heavenly help of Brother Love, which brought the world the most soul-sanctifying sermon yet in the gospel according to Neil. As opposed to his recent singles, "Brother Love's Traveling Salvation Show" connected almost immediately upon its release in February. It peaked at #22, making it Diamond's biggest hit since "Kentucky Woman" almost a year and a half earlier, an eternity in the pop music world of that era.

The original version of the *Brother Love's Traveling Salvation Show* album released in 1969—with Diamond appearing on the cover wearing a beard *and* love beads—was an effective, varied collection of tracks Diamond recorded with the American Sound team, and other tracks produced by Diamond himself or in collaboration with Tom Catalano. With Cogbill and Moman behind the board, he recorded "Glory Road," a hitchhiker's guide to the universe and an exquisite composition the very title of which reflected the rarified path on which Diamond now found himself traveling more freely. "And the Grass Won't Pay No Mind," produced by Diamond and Tom Catalano, was Diamond at his most poetically seductive as a singer and a songwriter. Speaking of the song, Neil would note that it was "pure stream of consciousness written more to capture a moment in time than to tell a story." Diamond would follow this approach more in the years to come.

The *Brother Love* album initially went as high as #82 on the top two hundred, but a single that Diamond wrote and recorded during his return trip to Memphis in May of 1969 would result in an even more universal classic.

By this time American Sound was on fire. Elvis Presley had made himself right at home and recorded "Suspicious Minds," "In the Ghetto," and "Kentucky Rain," songs that restored much of his long-squandered luster. In *Careless Love*, the second part of Peter Guralnick's brilliant biography of Elvis Presley, session trumpet player Wayne Jackson is quoted regarding the general feeling among the players upon the King's arrival: "I mean we were thrilled about Elvis, but it wasn't like doing Neil Diamond," Jackson said. That sentence alone is enough to confirm that by 1969 Neil Diamond himself had arrived in the eyes of his peers.

Now in a Memphis hotel room, Diamond found himself in his natural environment, playing on a guitar, trying to come up with a third song to work on during the next day's recording session. For many years, Neil would keep the closely guarded secret that the title "Sweet Caroline" was inspired by his memory of a picture of the young Caroline Kennedy he had once seen.

Diamond says that "Sweet Caroline" just seemed to come out of "the excitement of the moment." More specifically, Diamond's excitement seemed to focus on a chord in the song's "touching hands" section, a relatively unusual A6 chord that he had never played before. "It was probably one of the reasons it was such a big hit." Whatever the reason, "Sweet Caroline" would be a song that struck, and continues to strike, a particularly resounding chord around the world.

"Sweet Caroline," which Neil produced with Tommy Cogbill and Tom Catalano, may be the single most beloved and irresistible recording in Diamond's catalog of hits. The song returned Diamond to the top ten, hitting #4 on the singles chart and #3 on the Adult Contemporary chart. As if that wasn't enough, "Sweet Caroline" also became a sizable international hit, bringing Neil Diamond's good name and sound to the world.

Diamond has acknowledged just how much the popularity of "Sweet Caroline" meant to him, not just professionally, but personally. "There are very few places in the world that I can go where 'Sweet Caroline' is not known," Diamond said. "It makes you feel that all the work, and the time and all the stupid things you've done over your life and your career, has a little bit of meaning because it's touched *some* people."

Though the Boston Red Sox fans eventually adopted it as their anthem, "Sweet Caroline" is a song that belongs to everyone. Everybody from Frank Sinatra to Elvis Presley to Waylon Jennings would record "Sweet Caroline" over the years. Diamond has said that even Bob Dylan recorded the song—and sent him a copy for his personal listening pleasure.

Diamond says that these sorts of high-profile cover versions of his songs meant a great deal to him. "So maybe that helps to ease the criticism a little bit, that my peers accept me and respect me, and that's enough," Diamond said. Neil went on to add that Old Blue Eye's recording of "Sweet Caroline" was perhaps his favorite cover version ever of one of his songs. "Sinatra did 'Sweet Caroline' with a swing band, and he killed the song," Diamond said. "I mean, he just did it better than anybody, including me, ever did. I love that."

The massive success of "Sweet Caroline" was such that eventually it was added to a reissue of the *Brother Love* album, which featured a new album cover with Diamond clean shaven as well as a new title, *Brother Love's Traveling Salvation Show/Sweet Caroline.*

If Neil Diamond's fresh start at Uni Records got off to a frustratingly slow start, the momentum was now turning in his favor in a significant way, far bigger than anything he had yet experienced. The sixties had begun for Diamond as a student in New York City still trying to decide if he dared to pursue a life in music rather than some more certain and stable career. Somewhere in the middle of the decade he had, perhaps rashly, made some painful choices, for himself and for others he loved, as he moved on to a new life on another coast. Though he would remain close to his daughters, there was, inevitably, a sense of loss and of failure.

By the end of the sixties, Diamond was very busy, and far too focused on his music to spend much time ruminating over regrets. For him personally, it was a time of great happiness, and professionally, it was also a period of extraordinary achievement. Neil Diamond's last big hit of the sixties was at the top of the charts, just as he and Marcia were married on December 4, 1969. The song was called "Holly Holy," and once again it found Diamond preaching his own musical gospel on a truly radiant song of songs, one marked by an appealing sense of mystery and the presence of a rousing gospel choir. "Holly Holy" would feature a grand string arrangement by Lee Holdridge, who would soon become another of Diamond's significant regular musical collaborators.

Speaking to the BBC, Diamond once confessed that "Holly Holy" was "a weird song" that not even he could quite explain. Then, of course, he went on to explain the song exceedingly well when he added, "What I tried to do was create a religious experience between a man and a woman, as opposed to a man and a god."

As wonderfully weird as it is, "Holly Holy" soon followed "Sweet Caroline" into the top ten, rising all the way to #6 in November of 1969. With another sizable hit now in their hands, Uni quickly put together *Touching You, Touching Me,* named in honor of the unending popularity of "Sweet Caroline." The album included a few excellent originals such as "New York Boy," a charming autobiographical tale of a Brooklyn boy in the American South, and the far more poetic "And the Singer Sings His Songs."

Touching You, Touching Me also found Diamond recording a number of cover versions of notable songs by other great songwriters of the era. Diamond offered convincing interpretations of "Both Sides Now" by Joni Mitchell, "Everybody's Talkin'" by Fred Neil, "Until It's Time for You to Go" by Buffy Sainte-Marie, and "Mr. Bojangles" by Jerry Jeff Walker. And with this record, Neil Diamond would finally find his way into the top forty on the *Billboard* album chart, reaching #30. After years of struggle, and then daring to stand up for himself and start all over again at Uni, this rush of success was all heady stuff. And yet there were far more heady days ahead for Neil Diamond.

As the sixties ended, Diamond's strongly rooted belief in his own songs was finally paying off as he found himself what looked like the role of a lifetime. With the seventies now directly in front of him, Neil Diamond was walking down a glory road of his own making and wondering where it would take him next.

Song Sung 7

LOST BETWEEN TWO SHORES AND FOUND ON A HOT AUGUST NIGHT

L.A.'s fine but it ain't home

New York's home but it ain't mine no more

—"I AM . . . I SAID" BY NEIL DIAMOND

IN 1991, JUST A FEW YEARS AFTER I FIRST MET NEIL DIAMOND, I FOUND myself following his path from New York City to Los Angeles, a journey both external and internal that he sang about with great eloquence and poetic gravitas in "I Am . . . I Said," the same song that inspired the title of this book.

On advice of counsel, let me now state formally for the record that in going west as a not so young man, I was in no way seeking to stalk Neil Diamond. As evidence in this pleading, let the record now show that it was in fact Jann Wenner, my boss at *Rolling Stone*, who suggested that I make this big move after checking out my even bigger hotel bill from a two-week 1990 stay at the Sunset Marquis hotel, during which I ended up doing cover stories on Winona Ryder and Sinead

O'Connor, and interviewing another one of my all-time heroes, Joni Mitchell. Ladies and gentlemen of the jury, how on earth was I to know that your finer hotels actually *charged* for such things as long-distance telephone phone calls and food?

Perhaps looking to save on such travel expenses, Jann generously offered me the chance to relocate on the magazine's dime and head up *Rolling Stone*'s Los Angeles office editorially as his bureau chief, an honor that seemed ever so slightly less impressive once I realized that I would also be the only one from the editorial department in said bureau.

Having just recently broken up with a woman who also worked at *Rolling Stone*'s home office in New York, there was something suddenly appealing about putting at least 2,462 miles of distance between myself and just about everyone and everything I knew and loved. Also I liked the nice weather and the Chinese chicken salads. The only real hurdle to overcome in becoming a Los Angeleno was the embarrassing fact that despite being way in the back half of my twenties, I still did not know how to drive.

Truth be told, I had failed my first driver's test years earlier due to an honest disagreement between the New Jersey state tester and myself. He felt that the laws of the Garden State required that I, like every other properly licensed man and woman, actually stop at a stop sign. At the time, apparently, I felt otherwise. In Manhattan, not driving had proven to be no problem whatsoever. In Los Angeles, however, not driving was not practical, if not downright un-American. After all, there are absolutely no great Beach Boys songs about getting around by cab.

In order to expedite my transition to becoming *Rolling Stone*'s much loved and deeply tanned bureau chief, the magazine thoughtfully paid for me to take a crash course in driving, an unfortunate phrase, perhaps, but quite fitting all the same. Learning to drive in New York City is perhaps the only act of bravery that I have ever committed. My driving instructor, a charming and confident African American gentleman in his forties, instantly sized me up on the curb the first day and realized that I was the challenge of a lifetime. "I'm taking you *straight* to Harlem," he said soon after picking me up outside my apartment on Eighty-fifth Street and Amsterdam. As he explained it, I'd have "more room to learn" uptown.

Within just a few weeks, my teacher had done the impossible, and I passed my driving test, if not exactly with flying colors. Just days later, I flew to Los Angeles to begin my new first-class life among rock stars, movie stars, and others who I prayed would, like Neil Diamond, immediately recognize my fundamental *menschy* quality and embrace me as one of their own.

Like the narrator of "I Am . . . I Said," I was just some frog from New York who dreamed of changing location and becoming a king. Unlike Neil Diamond, sadly, I had no talent to speak of and I actually looked like a frog and not a particularly dashing amphibian at that. Still, with considerable pride, I report that just shy of my thirtieth birthday, I safely made the very first solo drive of my life in a rental car from Los Angeles International Airport to the Sunset Marquis Hotel, where I would stay for a week until I found a more permanent dwelling.

In those first few solitary days, I would rise every morning before dawn and drive all the way from West Hollywood to the Pacific coast in Malibu, arriving just as the sun was coming up over a beach that looked just like the one Diamond sits on alone on the cover of *Jonathan Livingston Seagull*. Then I would park, have breakfast, and drive back inland to start my day of work. During these long pleasure drives, I would listen to great West Coast music in the car to celebrate my new surroundings: The Beach Boys' *Pet Sounds*, Joni Mitchell's *Court and Spark*, The Eagles' *Hotel California*, Jane's Addiction's *Nothing's Shocking*, and, yes, Neil Diamond's classic *Hot August Night* live album recorded at the Greek Theatre.

Such was my sunny if solitary introduction to my new, free life. Traveling that long distance each morning, it didn't take long before I encountered my first coastal disturbance. Driving down the Pacific Coast Highway one morning, I noticed a light on the dashboard indicating that something was wrong. Let God and Al Gore forgive me, covering so much ground for no good reason, I had run through my first tank of free rental car gas. Even I knew that the tank needed to be filled. The only problem was that I had absolutely no idea how this was done. This was *not* something my instructor had covered during our crash course in Harlem, perhaps for safety reasons.

I had never felt more alone, more lost

"I am," I said, to no one there

And no one heard at all

Not even the rental car chair

Okay, so maybe I *didn't* say that, but I wish now I had. The crisis Neil Diamond sings about in "I Am . . . I Said" was existential; mine, far more practical and pitiful.

After literally seconds of thought, I pulled over and found the closest pay phone and called the only friend I had in Los Angeles, another rock critic named Steve Pond, who had far more driving and life experience. Steve very sweetly offered to jump in his car and give me one final and, as it turned out, crucial driving lesson: how to fill your own gas tank.

If Steve had not done so, I might very well be standing there by the Pacific Ocean right now, leaving me lonely still. And I'm not a man who likes to swear, but goddamn it, I've never cared for the sound of being alone.

In American culture, the 1970s were a period of great art, great self-indulgence, and my bar mitzvah, not necessarily in that order. Blame it on Richard Nixon or on the increased distribution of pot, but something was definitely in the air. Fortunately, it comes through powerfully and safely in the great film and music of the era.

The first year of the seventies saw the release of two new Neil Diamond albums that reflected his rapid growth artistically and commercially.

The first was a live album called *Gold,* recorded at Doug Weston's Troubadour, an intimate and popular venue in West Hollywood. *Gold* was recorded during an appearance in January 1970 for which the duo Seals and Crofts appeared as Neil's opening act. By cutting his first live album, Diamond could now reclaim many of his past Bang classics with rousing live versions of "Solitary Man," "Cherry, Cherry," "Kentucky Woman," and "Thank the Lord for the Night Time," all appearing here alongside some of Diamond's more recent Uni material like "Holly Holy," "Sweet Caroline," and "Brother Love's Traveling Salvation Show." Just before an explosive, show-concluding version of "Brother Love," Diamond performs a song he identifies as, surprisingly, his favorite that he's written to date—"And the Singer Sings His Song"—a sweet and delicate ballad that speaks to the very act of making and enjoying music in the presence of others.

Decidedly less sweet and delicate was a legal skirmish at this time that was an attempt to try and stop Diamond from releasing new live versions of his past Bang hits on *Gold.* In the end, Diamond won this battle too, and Bang's latest rerelease of "Solitary Man," which now rose to #21, may have actually helped the chart performance of *Gold.* This single-disc live album brought Neil Diamond into the top ten of the *Billboard* album chart for the first time, yet one more indication of his impressive career trajectory at the start of the new decade.

Gold caught the tail end of Neil Diamond's relatively stripped-down days as a rough-and-ready club act. And though the album directly preceded Diamond's true golden age as a massive concert draw,

Gold documented a hot set with Diamond backed by his able road band, Carol Hunter on guitar, Randy Sterling on bass, and Eddie Rubin on drums, joined by three backup singers, Jessie Smith, Vanetta Fields, and Edna Hunter, as produced by Tom Catalano and recorded by Armin Steiner. Still, there are moments on *Gold* when one can hear the group struggling to recreate the big sound of Diamond's recent hits like "Holly Holy" and "Sweet Caroline." In the years to come, Neil Diamond's backing band would expand and evolve along with his rapidly growing live audience, but *Gold* nonetheless effectively presented a genuinely rocking night from a live performer who was turning into a real pro.

Rather than simply keep the momentum going with more of the same, Neil Diamond took this opportunity to record what was his boldest and riskiest album yet. For his next album, *Tap Root Manuscript*, he took a great leap forward into the musical unknown, composing and recording his first attempt at an extended piece arranged by jazz great Marty Paich. "The African Trilogy," as it would become known, paid tribute to African music from Diamond's unique perspective decades before world music hit the West. He took the task seriously, researching the subject through the Kenyan Mission and the United Nations in New York and with the African Studies department closer to home at UCLA.

The highlight of the "The African Trilogy" would become one of Diamond's least likely and most mesmerizing hits. "Soolaimon" was meant to be a variation on the word *salamah*, which Diamond explained in the liner notes for *In My Lifetime* could mean "hello" and "welcome" as well as "good-bye" and "peace be with you" in a variety of languages. In America, "Soolaimon" meant a wild top-thirty hit, an artistic triumph all the more remarkable when one considers Paul Simon would not release *Graceland*, his groundbreaking fusion of American and South

African sounds, for another decade and a half. While the chart placement for "Soolaimon" wasn't terribly high by Diamond's current standards, it becomes more impressive when you consider the challenging nature of the song. In concert, it would become an even bigger favorite and would often open Diamond's live set. Like "Brother Love's Traveling Salvation Show, " "Soolaimon" was more than a song—on a good night in concert, it became a religious experience.

That said, "Soolaimon" wasn't even the biggest hit on *Tap Root Manuscript*. In addition to the African-themed material, the album also featured a top-twenty cover of "He Ain't Heavy . . . He's My Brother," an uplifting pop standard that had recently become a smash for the Hollies, as well as Neil Diamond's first number-one pop hit as a recording artist.

"Cracklin' Rosie" is a testament to Diamond's genius not simply as a musical figure, but also as a communicator. Here is a song with truly strange subject matter that Diamond somehow turned into a contemporary pop perennial. Neil explained the inspiration of the song to me for *Rolling Stone* in 1988. The idea for "Cracklin' Rosie" came from a folk story that he had heard regarding an Indian tribe in northern Canada that had more men than women. On this reservation, Neil told me, "on Saturday nights when they go out, the guys all get their girl; the guys without girls get a girl called Crackin' Rosie, a bottle of Crackling Rose. That's their girl for the weekend. I heard this story and thought it was a great idea for a song."

Another songwriter of the era coming across this tale might have been inspired to write a depressing protest song about the dangers of alcoholism, or alternatively, an equally depressing protest song about the worrying lack of women in certain sections of the Great White North. In Diamond's hands, this mildly distressing tale was somehow transformed into one of the most joyful and infectious recordings of all time. If you don't believe it, find a copy of "Cracklin' Rosie" and play it now, play it now, play it *now*.

With an excellent arrangement by jazz pianist Don Randi, "Cracklin' Rosie" is simply undeniable. For his part, Diamond paints an equally evocative lyrical picture. As a child, I could not help but sing along with every word of the song, even the part about Rosie being a "store-bought woman," which sounded far more filthy before I knew that it was liquor Diamond was singing about.

Further proving that Diamond now possessed the artistic freedom that he sought, *Tap Root Manuscript* also featured another fascinating and revealing track called "Done Too Soon," an unusual song that he wrote, perhaps not coincidentally, during a particularly bumpy plane flight. "Done Too Soon" dealt with mortality in an extremely creative way. Years before Billy Joel took a similar approach for "We Didn't Start the Fire," Diamond covered a remarkable amount of historical ground by essentially presenting a list of notable figures. "Done Too Soon" spotlighted a wide range of celebrated men and women in history who shared the fact that they all died young. Beginning with "Jesus Christ, Fanny Brice," the song went on to include everyone from the famed publisher Henry Luce to Lincoln assassin John Wilkes Booth, from the great Yiddish writer Sholom Aleichem to controversial death penalty recipient Caryl Chessman.

"It was kind of esoteric, especially at that time," Diamond once told me. "But it's just me trying to say something a little different, just try and jog something in a person's memory, or to elicit a reaction. That's what my job is, to do something a little bit different, and yet something that's me and something that's you."

The most creative and edifying example of extreme name-dropping in the history of the entertainment business, "Done Too Soon" proved that Diamond was now powerful enough to bring "Karl and Chico

Marx" to #65 on the pop charts. Such was the success of *Tap Root Manuscript* that even the rock press sounded an almost welcoming note. As a double review of that album and *Gold* in *Rolling Stone* began, "If groups are a thing of the past, and the solo artist has again come into prominence, then maybe Neil Diamond's time has come."

Few songs divide the world of Neil Diamond and non–Neil Diamond fans as strongly as the one at the heart of his next album, 1971's *Stones'* "I Am . . . I Said." The spark for the wildly successful song came one afternoon following Diamond's failed screen test to play the famed rebel comedian Lenny Bruce, which would have been his film debut. Though he would have the title and some of the melody within an hour, "I Am . . . I Said" would ultimately turn out to be the single most challenging and time-consuming song that he ever wrote.

"It took four months every day, all day," Neil once told me. "I'd go into my room, lock the door and I struggled with this song. It came out of a screen test that I did for a movie they were going to make on Lenny Bruce's life. And somehow I did one of the scenes in the morning, and I went back to my dressing room during lunch. I was really depressed, 'cause I knew I had done a miserable job. And I had my guitar there, and I started to play this thing, which within fifteen minutes started to have a title. And it had that line about the frog who dreamed about being a king. So I went in every day and I fought with it. I cursed it out. It was like a person who wouldn't submit. I got as close as I could get."

In his 1976 *Rolling Stone* interview with Ben Fong-Torres, Diamond even suggested that attempting to channel Lenny Bruce had another big impact on his life. "I went into therapy almost immediately after that," he explained. "Because there were things coming out of me that I couldn't deal with. It was frightening because I had never been willing to admit this part of my personality."

The song that started coming out of Diamond that afternoon of the screen test gave voice to all his feelings of self-doubt and his growing sense of isolation. Nearly a decade later, when we spoke about the song again for the liner notes of *In My Lifetime*, Diamond once again emphasized how important the process of writing the song was to him. "I knew it had great potential and I was unwilling to accept anything but the raw truth in the lyrics. It was a daily battle to put that song and those sentiments on paper, but when it was done, it turned out to be one of the most satisfying songs I had ever written."

Diamond's interest in film seemed to be growing at this time. There were rumors that he would take the James Dean role in a remake of *Rebel Without a Cause*, a project that sounds slightly insane in retrospect, but would certainly have provided an excellent forum for brooding on the big screen. And Diamond did form a small production company and option the rights to *Death at an Early Age*, Jonathan Kozol's powerful, National Book Award–winning account of his first year teaching at an inner-city Boston school in the sixties.

The film for which Diamond made his big screen test that inspired "I Am . . . I Said" was never made, though a few years later a separate project about Lenny Bruce was made by director Bob Fosse with the great Dustin Hoffman in the lead role, a part for which he was nominated for an Academy Award. Here's the part that you are hereby free to disregard, though I feel the need to share it with you. While I was producing Neil Diamond's episode of *Behind the Music*, we again discussed the experience of that screen test and what it meant to him. Clearly, it had been traumatic enough to inspire the identity crisis at the heart of "I Am . . . I Said," and I asked if there was any way I could see the screen test for myself.

Neil, who likes to control his work as carefully as the next guy, and perhaps a lot more, was generous enough to locate the original screen test and let us include a snippet of it in our show. Now, I will tell you all day long—and I am—that Neil Diamond is one of our greatest singer-songwriters and has been for decades. I would not make the same claim for the man as an actor, mostly because he's done relatively little in this medium. That said, Diamond's Lenny Bruce screen test shocked me because in just a few moments, he somehow transformed himself into a believable dirty-mouthed, Constitution-defending co-median. Not exactly an obvious example of type casting. Now, I'm not saying that Neil's Lenny Bruce would have been necessarily *better* than Dustin Hoffman's. Suffice to say, if I were the executive in charge, I would have immediately offered Diamond the role, and "I Am . . . I Said" might never have been written.

For the record, there are good people with bad taste who might have much preferred that scenario. The popular humor writer Dave Barry once wrote a column claiming that "I Am . . . I Said" is one of the worst lyrics ever written, and then wrote *The Book of Bad Songs*, a tome that Barry then dedicated to Diamond. In a 2006 interview with *Time* magazine, Barry told Jeff Chu that Diamond had a "surprisingly nice" reaction to this slight, inviting Barry to attend one of his con-certs in South Florida. "I didn't go," Barry told *Time*, "because (a) I couldn't and (b) he might have had people kill me."

"I Am . . . I Said" was released as a single with "Done Too Soon" on the flip side, and peaked at #4 on the *Billboard* charts in May of 1971. That same year, the song would appear twice on Diamond's 1971 album *Stones,* which also featured Diamond singing a number of excellent cover versions of outstanding compositions by Joni Mitchell ("Chelsea Morn-ing"), Leonard Cohen ("Suzanne"), and Tom Paxton ("The Last Thing on My Mind"). Best of all was Diamond's strong, stately interpretation of Randy Newman's brilliant song "I Think It's Going to Rain Today."

Stones also featured a far more lighthearted but still entirely delicious song inspired by the healthier food habits Diamond was exposed to in his new life in Los Angeles, "Crunchy Granola Suite." In the liner notes to *In My Lifetime,* Diamond explained that when he wrote the song he was "newly transported to California and was impressed by the health food consciousness there. I actually thought 'Crunchy Granola Suite' might change people's eating habits!" Diamond may have fallen short on that honorable goal, but he could take comfort in the fact that in "Crunchy Granola Suite," which hit #14 on the charts, paired on a single with *Stones*' title track, he had managed to write the coolest song ever written about granola or any other breakfast food made of rolled oats, nuts, and honey.

Diamond's next studio album, 1972's *Moods,* featured his second number-one hit, "Song Sung Blue," the bounciest chart-topper ever to be inspired by Mozart's *Piano Concerto no. 21.* "This is one to which I never paid too much attention," Diamond says. "A very basic message, unadorned. I didn't even write a bridge to it . . . I had no idea that it would be a huge hit or that people would want to sing along with it."

In 1988, Diamond told me that "Song Sung Blue" wasn't even his first choice for a single from the *Moods* album. As he recalled, Russ Regan, who ran Uni and brought him to the label, pushed hard for "Song Sung Blue," telling Diamond, "It's going to be your biggest copyright ever." Despite his own doubts, Diamond smartly listened to Regan and was very glad that he did. "Although the lyric says everything I wanted it to say, there's not much meat to it, you know? But it turned out to be a major, major copyright." In the years to come, everyone from the Scottish punk band Altered Images to Andy Williams, as well as Frank Sinatra, Bobby Darin, and Wayne Newton, would record "Song Sung Blue."

Moods, which also included the top-twenty hits "Walk on Water" and "Play Me," rose to #5, the exact same position as would the live album that more than any other solidified Diamond's place in music in the mid-seventies, *Hot August Night*.

In the summer of 1971, Neil Diamond played seven sold-out nights at the prestigious Greek Theatre, an atmospheric venue nestled inside the city's Griffith Park. The next summer he would return for another ten sold-out shows during which he would record the live album that would close out his deal with MCA's Uni. After an intense bidding war between Columbia and Warner Bros., Diamond would sign what was the biggest record deal in music for a brief time, for a rumored $4 million advance.

If Diamond was moving on once again to a new corporate home, he definitely did so in high style, with an album that saw him backed by not just his current backing band—Dennis St. John on drums, Richard Bennett on guitar, Emory Gordy Jr. on guitars and vibes, Jefferson Kewley on percussion, Alan Lindgren on keyboards, Danny Nicholson on guitar, Reine Press on bass—but also a full thirty-five-piece string orchestra.

The excitement was such that Diamond not only sold out the Greek for the entire run, but also drew more frugal and enthusiastic sorts to climb trees surrounding the theater so they could see the show— the "tree people," they were called.

"Thank you people in the audience, the pays," Diamond announces early on *Hot August Night*. "Tree people out there, god bless you, I'm singing for you too."

Whoever he was singing for at the Greek on that hot August night, Diamond gave a performance to be remembered, and one that millions have remembered ever since thanks to that double album. By the end of 1972, *Hot August Night* was on its way to becoming one of the most successful live albums of all time, and one of Diamond's most popular recordings ever, spending seventy-eight weeks on the *Billboard* charts.

In 2001, Neil Diamond said that *Hot August Night* forever captures "a very special show for me. We went all out to knock 'em dead in L.A." Listen to the album, and you can hear Diamond doing exactly that. *Hot August Night* further marked the arrival of Neil Diamond as a charismatic concert attraction with moves all his own. Look at the cover of *Hot August Night* and there's an image of the once shy performer becoming something else entirely.

When I interviewed him for *Behind the Music*, Jack Black rightly identified Diamond as being part of "the showman school of rock and roll." Breaking down Diamond's appeal as a live performer even more specifically for me, Black identified and recreated one of Diamond's patented stage moves. "He's kind of like, it's like a *loveslinger*," Black explained. "He's slinging *love*."

Diamond was now ready and able to return to Columbia Records, the same company that had quickly dropped him from the label more than a decade earlier. Diamond was returning under far more attractive terms. He did so just as his career was hitting a new peak—he was slinging his fans lots of love and they were slinging even more right back.

As 1973 began, the frog, if he indeed ever *was* a frog, was wearing a crown.

Song Sung 8

OF BEING AND
BIRD DROPPINGS

Lost
On a painted sky
Where the clouds are hung
For the poet's eye

—"BE," BY NEIL DIAMOND

FACED WITH THE ENVIABLE QUANDARY OF HOW TO FOLLOW UP AN overwhelming popular and critical success like the concerts that produced *Hot August Night*, Diamond made a brilliant move when he decided it was time to play Broadway. Then he made an extremely dramatic exit from public life, stage left.

On October 3, 1972, Diamond kicked off his first of twenty soldout performances at Broadway's famed Winter Garden Theater. Built in 1896 to house the American Horse Exchange, the building was redesigned and reopened as the elegant Winter Garden Theater in 1911. Over the years, this relatively small but legendary theater on the east side of Broadway between Fiftieth and Fifty-first streets has been a home to such historic shows as *Peter Pan*, *West Side Story*, *Funny Girl*, *Mame*, *Follies*, *Gypsy*, *Beatlemania*, *42nd Street*, *Cats* for nearly twenty years, and most recently *Mamma Mia!* Yet for a short but meaningful time in 1972, somewhere between runs of *Follies* and *Gypsy*, the Winter Garden would become the impressive home to one of the greatest shows on earth—Neil Diamond in concert.

For any New York boy, even one now living large in Los Angeles, playing Broadway was the most glamorous sort of homecoming imaginable. For Diamond, this was also one hell of a dramatic way of returning to Tin Pan Alley in style, as one of music's reigning superstars. Reportedly, Diamond was the first solo concert performer on Broadway since Al Jolson, another popular entertainer of some note and the star of a 1927 movie called *The Jazz Singer*, a title that would also figure very prominently in Diamond's life in years to come.

Playing Broadway proved to be a very significant and even thrilling moment for Diamond, but in a sense it also marked the end of his first era as a performing sensation. As Neil told the *Los Angeles Times* at the time, "I figure after I finish at the Winter Garden, I'll have satisfied an old ambition. I'll have played every historic theater I ever wanted to." The shows were, even by Diamond's own standards, highly emotional affairs played out before not just new fans, but old friends and family, including my parents. "My name is Neil," he told his audience from the stage, "I weep. I cry. I care . . ."

A man with a flair for the dramatic, Diamond chose this moment of personal and professional triumph to announce that he would take an extended sabbatical from touring at the end of his big Broadway debut. Diamond's stated intention was to spend more time with his family, including he and his wife Marcia's first son Jesse. Considering the furious professional pace that he had been keeping during the previous decade, Diamond needed to catch his breath and consider where he had been and where he was going. And so he took a breather. In the years that would follow, Diamond has often said stepping out of the spotlight was one of the wisest decisions of his life.

Originally, Diamond's self-enforced retirement from the road was supposed to last a year or so, but in the end, it would last forty months.

"I left for about four years really," Neil said. "Did very little but spend time with my kids and write a few songs. I think it was one of the happiest times in my life. No pressure from business. It gave me a chance to know myself as an adult in a way that I never had before. I think it was the most important part of my life in the last thirty years."

Having reached this high point, Neil Diamond was now sufficiently on top of the world to feel comfortable taking the time for himself and his loved ones. Having already blown one marriage in his first rush toward success, Diamond was now willing to try and examine his priorities and just about everything else in his life. At age thirty-one, he had already enjoyed more than twenty top-forty hits, but he knew well that success had not come for free.

"When you're as involved and as passionate about what you're doing as I was, it seems like everything else took a second position," Neil told me. "You do pay a price in your personal life, and I paid that price time and time again." Knowing that his loved ones inevitably paid that same price along with him, Diamond made a change.

First, Diamond agreed to play one last, nonpaying gig: a benefit performance for George McGovern's presidential campaign and the Robert Kennedy Memorial Fund, hosted by Ethel Kennedy and Eunice Kennedy Shriver at Timberlawn, the Shriver estate in Rockville, Maryland. In an often repeated story that suggests that Diamond now had fans in high places making requests, Mrs. Kennedy is said to have poured beer on Neil when he chose to play Mrs. Shriver's favorite song, "Sweet Caroline," before Mrs. Kennedy's preference, "New York Boy."

This was the last song request that Neil would have to worry about taking for quite a while. He then retired from the road and returned to Los Angeles, where he had homes inland in Holmby Hills and by the sea in Malibu. Settling into a more domestic existence, he would reclaim his family life, read great books, and stare at the Pacific. The music business, he has often said, was always in a rush, but Diamond would no longer allow the business to set the pace of his life for him.

Yet to anyone who has ever met or followed his career, the idea of Neil Diamond not writing songs seems unimaginable. Before very long, he had agreed to begin to make good on his new contract with Columbia Records in one of the least predictable ways imaginable: giving voice to a bird.

That said, this wasn't just *any* bird for whom Neil Diamond was going to sing, but rather an imaginary bird that had recently become a legitimate pop superstar in his own right: Jonathan Livingston Seagull. Written by Richard Bach, *Jonathan Livingston Seagull* was a small fable that became a massive publishing phenomenon. Published in 1970, there were a million copies in print by the end of 1972 as the small book topped the *New York Times* best-seller list for thirty-eight weeks.

"*Everybody* read Jonathan Seagull," Neil said. "It was a philosophical, flimsy little thing about a seagull who just wouldn't follow the crowd."

After catching Diamond in all his glory at the Greek Theatre in 1971, Hall Bartlett, the director-producer of the film version of *Jonathan Livingston Seagull,* had become a big fan of Diamond and aggressively pursued him to provide a musical liftoff for the movie. Initially, Neil passed on this unusual offer from the veteran filmmaker, whose previous credits included *Zero Hour!* with Dana Andrews and Sterling Hayden and *All the Young Men* with Alan Ladd and Sidney Poitier. These were, one hesitates only slightly to add, all movies that starred human beings and not birds.

"I didn't have the vaguest idea how to write songs from a seagull's point of view," Diamond explained in the liner notes for *In My Lifetime*. "So I turned it down. Then I thought a little more and decided to do it. I figured nobody else had more insight into writing for a seagull, so why not?"

Arguably, despite his obvious liability of being a human being and not a winged creature, Neil Diamond was actually well suited for the gig. In a sense, Diamond was the perfect choice. Like the movie's title bird, Neil had always been something of a loner with his own strong sense of direction. His career was testament to his tendency to fly his own way and leave the flock behind. After all, any man who could write "Shilo" for an imaginary friend appeared to have as good a shot as anyone of writing songs successfully for a seagull.

Furthermore, by this time in his career, Diamond's work was increasingly evincing a philosophical, spiritual side with elements of self-help that were quickly becoming part of a movement in the New Age of the seventies. Right from "Solitary Man" on, Neil Diamond had demonstrated a natural tendency to look within and create songs that expressed his inner life.

"Neil is very, very sensitive, I think," Ellie Greenwich said. "He's very into himself, his feelings, and what he's all about. And I think Neil turns to Neil to solve all his problems and to deal with life. He *is* a solitary man."

Greenwich's ex-husband and musical partner, Jeff Barry, sounded a little less forgiving when he spoke to Ben Fong-Torres in *Rolling Stone* in 1976. Torres offered his own view that "while many of Diamond's songs deal directly with loneliness, love and the healing power of music, many others are elliptical, if you know what I mean." He then quoted Jeff Barry as saying of his former partner and protégé, "His songs haven't changed, really; they just get harder to understand."

Diamond understood that he faced a new sort of challenge here, and he did not go into *Jonathan Livingston Seagull* flying blind. He told Robert Hilburn in the *Los Angeles Times* that he approached two of the great film composers in the world, Henry Mancini and Lalo Schifrin, in order to get a more full understanding of what the job of scoring a movie involved. Both of the film music greats assured Neil that if he would make his music then the rest would follow. "They took away the doubts," Diamond said. "I'm indebted to them both."

Diamond went on to say that he threw himself into this project "as completely as I ever had before." Because *Jonathan Livingston Seagull* was a spiritual story, Diamond explained that he had to do some soul searching of his own to understand the spiritual nature of his high-flying character. It would be six months of exploring various spiritual approaches to life before Diamond would have the breakthrough that led to the song "Be."

On tracks like "Be"—literally a six-minute flight of pure existentialism— "Skybird," and "Lonely Looking Sky," among others, Diamond managed to do what some might consider the impossible: he got in touch with his inner seagull.

In *Behind the Music*, Diamond had nothing bad to say about his extended time spent creating the music for *Jonathan Livingston Seagull*. "The process itself—the writing and the understanding that you had to come to—was also an interesting part of my life, and also reflects part of my idea of self-improvement and, you know, moving on and not necessarily traveling with the flock. It was a great experience."

As it would turn out, *Jonathan Livingston Seagull* was emphatically *not* a great experience for most critics who were paid to see it. Reviewing the movie for the *Chicago Sun Times*, Roger Ebert confessed that he had actually walked out of the movie, but not before he had seen quite enough to declare, "This has got to be the biggest pseudocultural, would-be metaphysical ripoff of the year."

Even with what some acknowledged as the movie's beautiful cinematography, few critics could suspend disbelief once the gulls in the movie started to speak in the voices of James Franciscus, Hal Holbrook, and Juliet Mills. In the book, capturing the inner monologues of a seagull had seemed like a charming device; on the silver screen it was widely judged to be a complete and utter failure.

And so despite the overwhelming success of the book, the film version of *Jonathan Livingston Seagull* would prove to be an almost total bust as the bird's box office plummeted precipitously to the earth. Beyond the bad business and the negative reviews, author Richard Bach actually sued to block the film's release at one point. Diamond too would eventually engage in some legal maneuvers to protect his musical contributions. What had once seemed destined to become a film for the ages had sadly turned out to be more dog than high-flying bird.

Still, Neil Diamond would somehow break from this whole flock of failure as his *Jonathan Livingston Seagull* sound track album went on to become one of the best-selling albums of his career, all without the benefit of a major hit single. Diamond's score, with contributions by Lee Holdridge, would also win a Golden Globe and a Grammy. Diamond won his first and to date only Grammy for best instrumental composition written specifically for a motion picture or for television. Actor Richard Harris, of *McArthur Park* musical fame, himself won a separate Grammy at the same time for the *Jonathan* spoken word album.

As Diamond's music grew more and more introspective and searching, his audience now seemed inclined to follow anywhere he would dare to take them. So while *Jonathan Livingston Seagull* fell to earth, the rise of Neil's latest album was downright phoenixlike. "Be," a fine dramatic musical statement, if far from an obvious pop radio single, managed to climb into the top forty with some difficulty, hitting as high as #34 on the *Billboard* pop singles chart, while another single, "Skybird," made it only as far as #75. Still, the *Jonathan Livingston Seagull* sound track album itself would hit #2 and stay in flight on the charts for the better part of a year.

True confessions time here: I have very happily listened to the *Jonathan Livingston Seagull* album many times over the years. I still own the sound track on eight-track and reel-to-reel tape, despite no longer having any mechanism on which to play either one of them. Yet as much of a hardcore Diamondhead as I am proud to be, I had, until the spring of 2008, never seen the movie even once.

When *Jonathan Livingston Seagull* first came out, I was twelve and thus not yet man enough to make my own moviegoing decisions. Apparently the bad buzz on this birdbrained feature film had reached even our home in Tenafly, New Jersey, and my parents refused to take me. Ever since that first short run, it has frankly been exceptionally easy to avoid the film, since poor *Jonathan* has never quite entered the pantheon of past film classics. And as much as I love Neil Diamond, I never felt the need to see the movie when the songs themselves were all I needed to get inside the head of a seagull. Put the album on, close your eyes, and it's quite a good movie in its own right.

The closest I came to taking a flyer and seeing *Jonathan Livingston Seagull* came during one of Diamond's concert tours a few years back when he revisited a segment of songs from his sound track album, backed by what I could only assume was footage from the original movie projected behind him. Perhaps because the seagulls were seen and not heard talking in this instance, I now felt emotionally prepared to break from the flock and finally give *Jonathan* a chance myself.

Then as fate would have it, in late 2007 *Jonathan Livingston Seagull* was finally released on DVD by Paramount. Online one day after

Googling "Neil Diamond," I happened to catch a review of the DVD by Matthew Hays in the *Montreal Mirror*. Hays, while acknowledging the movie's tortured history, also fairly noted, "In its favor, *Jonathan Livingston Seagull* does offer some stunning cinematography. And it did receive awards for its sound track, written and sung by the only person I could imagine writing and singing a sound track for this movie: Neil Diamond."

And so for Neil's sake I decided that the time had come for me to confront my fears and actually watch the damned movie. Suddenly, it felt as if not having the nerve to face this talking seagull was becoming an albatross around my neck. Yet, this was too daunting a task for just one man, so like the abusive coward that I am, I forced my two sons, Andrew, ten, and Alec, eight, to sit and watch with me.

What follows, then, is the Wild family flight log of our very human shared misadventure with *Jonathan Livingston Seagull* in April 2008. For the record, my wife, Fran, wisely refused to have anything to do with this and decided to use her valuable time to do something far more productive and forward-thinking—go running on a treadmill.

Together the Wild boys began by looking at the *Jonathan Livingston Seagull* DVD cover and were somewhat encouraged by what we saw. Under the movie's familiar title, and beneath an illustration we assumed to be a gull, were words promising us the "Grammy Winning Score from Neil Diamond." Considering that we are a family of Diamond lovers, so far, so good. Beneath that, we were led to believe that this movie would be "A Film That Will Lift Your Spirits and Make Your Heart Soar."

Preparing ourselves to soar with our newly uplifted spirits, we then pressed play and sat back on the couch.

During the film's opening credits, played against an instrumental version of Neil Diamond's song "Be," I was very relieved to discover that I was in fact a responsible parent, because the film was rated "G" for general audience. Soon I would discover why a more fitting rating might be "N" for no audience whatsoever.

After enjoying a few moments of pretty, color footage of some clouds and impressive big waves, I felt encouraged. Perhaps I had been fearful of *Jonathan* all those years for no good reason. It was also nice to see that the film was dedicated "To the real Jonathan Livingston Seagull, who lives within us all." Then my youngest son, Alec, who tends to ask an unending series of questions that I can never answer, wondered aloud, "Daddy, did they have green screens then?" I let this film history question hang in the air just like a bird. Then together we all watched some rather lovely shots of the sea, and then we watched some more.

Perhaps suddenly noticing the extremely slow, serious, and *very* seventies pace of the film, my older son, Andrew, asked a question that was my first hint that this might not be the inspirational but fun-filled family movie that I had hoped. "Daddy," he said, "I wonder if I've ever seen a movie that *wasn't* comedy?" Somewhere in his ten-year-old soul, he sensed there were few laughs to be had here.

Our mood didn't brighten much as the boys and I witnessed seagulls feed furiously on some dead fish dropped off from a passing fishing boat. This feeding became a bloody battle for seagull sustenance. "They *really* want that fish!" Alec said, now clearly and sweetly trying to please his daddy by feigning the slightest interest in the proceedings.

As we watched images of a seagull flying against what looked like a dramatic sunrise, Alec thoughtfully added, "Wow, *cool* sun." Bravely or foolhardily, we pressed on, still following the bird's travels, as we were still shy of ten minutes into what the DVD cover suggested was a ninety-nine-minute film.

Our ears perked up in excitement when we heard Neil Diamond's voice ring out on the movie's sound track with "Be," the grand stream of consciousness about the search for meaning and about existence itself that had been his first breakthrough in writing the score. As the seagull we now presumed to be Jonathan Livingston himself took up a picturesque perch on a seaside cliff, Alec assured me that "this is a *good* song, Dad!" And indeed it is.

Then as Neil sang the lines "Holy, holy / Sanctus, sanctus" in an especially deep voice, Andrew offered some mild praise for what he was seeing. "Really good effects and pictures," he proclaimed, perhaps trying to rally our *Seagull* spirits. In that moment, I didn't have the heart to tell my son that those special effects he liked were mostly by God, or whoever else is the holy, holy one in charge of creating seagulls and colorful skies.

Then before even thirteen minutes had passed, it all fell apart for us as Jonathan started taking his most dramatic plunge yet and hit the water. Then that bird bastard did something far more unforgivable—he spoke.

In the curiously disconnected voice-over of James Franciscus, Jonathan Livingston Seagull started verbalizing apparently profound thoughts like, "Maybe seagulls can't fly faster than sixty-two miles per hour, but wouldn't it be *great* if we could?"

As a child myself, when I was roughly the same age as Alec, I had quite enjoyed Franciscus' performance in *Beneath the Planet of the Apes*. Yet now, his dialogue fell horribly flat for both me and my boys. The three of us looked at each other with a mixture of shock, horror, and the deepest sort of commiseration. In a flash, what looked like it might be a night watching a nice, trippy family nature movie together had become something else entirely. When Jonathan Livingston Seagull started talking, the movie suddenly seemed scarier than Hitchcock's *The Birds*.

We pressed on while Jonathan sought to talk things out with his seagull parents, who appeared bent on giving him some odd sort of guilt trip, as far as any of us could tell. Perhaps this sort of family *mishegas* was to be expected. After all, their last name *was* Seagull.

By now, my son Andrew had quietly curled up in a corner with a good book not written by Richard Bach, but instead by Eoin Colfer, author of the beloved *Artemis Fowl*. Alec, meanwhile, soldiered on, giving this whole strange *Seagull* thing his very best shot. He did so, I imagine, in part being a dutiful son and in part because he seemed endlessly fascinated that I was writing down his every word of reaction to the seemingly endless movie experience we were sharing.

Looking on the bright side, Alec continued to tell me that he liked the music he was hearing on the sound track. He asked me how long Neil Diamond had been writing music. I told him that Neil had been making music since roughly forty years before he was born in 1999.

"Wow," Alec said.

"Wow indeed," I answered.

Then ever so quietly, Alec slipped out of the room and went into the kitchen on a very meaningful and significant quest of his own: the search for dessert. His brother Andrew soon followed, and then suddenly, much like Jonathan Livingston Seagull himself, I found myself very much alone.

When the boys returned a few minutes later, I was nodding off a bit despite the fact that it was not late—it just *felt* that way. Refreshed, we all gave the bird one more final chance, but by now it was a nonstarter. "I have *no* idea what this bird's even talking about," Andrew said, and I was tempted to agree. Before they left the room again to do something—anything—else, Andrew did make one sweet attempt to sum up the message of Jonathan Livingston Seagull. "It's like, break away from the flock and you'll get killed. That's like . . . *Soviet!*"

Feeling a greater responsibility to you, my still imaginary flock of readers, to complete my own journey with Jonathan, I sought once again to stay on course, but by the time Jonathan Livingston Seagull appeared to be up on trial for some vague seagull crime, my resolve was slipping.

Just then the boys returned to our family room.

"Dad," Andrew said as if they had conferred, planning some sort of intervention. "Can we *please* watch *American Idol*?"

Though I was no fan of that show, and though it was Mariah Carey Week and Neil Diamond wouldn't make his first appearance there for a few weeks more, I could torture my sons no further. We turned off the *Jonathan Livingston Seagull* DVD, changed the channel, and settled in to watch some actual human beings and Simon Cowell. Almost instantly, we realized that hearing Simon speak was still far less disturbing than a talking seagull.

HELLO AGAIN

I've seen the light and I've seen the flame
And I've been this way before and I'm sure to be
this way again

— "I'VE BEEN THIS WAY BEFORE," BY NEIL DIAMOND

BEYOND DEFINITELY PROVING THAT BIRDS IN MOVIES SHOULD NOT speak unless spoken to, *Jonathan Livingston Seagull* established that Neil Diamond fans were a massive and faithful flock in their own right. Whatever well-deserved bricks the critics threw at *Jonathan*, Diamond's admirers were now established as true believers who zealously followed their own tastes, much as their musical hero himself had done throughout his career. Stunningly, Diamond's sound track for a major box-office bomb somehow became the single best-selling movie sound track album of all time, at least until *Saturday Night Fever* disco danced its way to the top in 1978, quickly selling more than ten million copies around the world.

Making his Columbia debut with such a project might have seemed like a fairly risky proposition, yet its tremendous success powerfully reinforced Diamond's unique power position in the music business. Just as Bang had done before them, MCA predictably capitalized on Diamond's popularity in 1974 with a new collection of the man's

Uni recordings called *His 12 Greatest Hits,* a collection of favorites that provided a fine, revenue-enhancing way for newcomers to the Neil Diamond party to join in all the fun. The album cover for *His 12 Greatest Hits,* featuring a movie star front cover portrait by famed photographer Harry Langdon, suggested that Neil Diamond, unlike Jonathan Livingston Seagull, was definitely ready for his close-up.

Clearly, the dire box-office performance of Hall Bartlett's film assured that there would be no *Jonathan Livingston Seagull II.* Yet in a sense, there was some sense of continuity, at least musically. One extremely strong, stately number that Diamond failed to finish in time for *Jonathan,* called "I've Been This Way Before," went on to became the powerful opening song on his next studio album, 1974's *Serenade.* As late as 1996, Diamond still spoke of "I've Been This Way Before" not making the *Jonathan Livingston Seagull* sound track as "one of my disappointments about the project." Indeed, to these human ears, "I've Been This Way Before" would have been a high point of the *Jonathan* sound track, just as it ended up being on *Serenade.*

"I've Been This Way Before," a song that effectively conjured up deep feelings of déjà vu and reincarnation, represented further proof that Diamond was doing considerable soul searching in his music as in his life. Neil was, of course, hardly the only one exploring far and wide spiritually back in the seventies. In a September 1973 interview with the *New York Times,* Diamond explained that his research for the film had been extensive and intense. "In my surge to understand what the *Jonathan Livingston* story was about, I got myself involved in philosophy and religion," Diamond said. "As a result, I began working with a yogi—as friend, student, teacher, that kind of relationship—for about six weeks, meeting every day." Diamond added that the impact of this spiritual inquiry was personal as well as professional. "I guess working on the music for the film really changed my life somewhat."

"I've Been This Way Before" suggested that Diamond's own spiritual searching could pay off for him, musically as well as personally. The *Serenade* album itself, however, felt somewhat transitional, as Diamond's songs seemed once again densely poetic and philosophically musing, as if the singer-songwriter were still at least partly up there in the clouds with Jonathan Livingston Seagull. Furthermore, having dealt with orchestral elements more than ever before while working on the sound track, some of Diamond's songs on *Serenade* felt almost overwhelmed by the album's lush production. Still, reviewing the album in *Rolling Stone*, Tom Nolan overstated things considerably when he wrote that "all that Diamond has to offer are bland musings adrift on an empty sea of strings."

Even by this point, Diamond could not have been entirely surprised by the tone of his naysayers. His relationship with the emerging rock press had already been mixed, and he had his own theories as to why this was. In an interview with Michael Ochs that appeared in the rock magazine *Crawdaddy* in 1971, Diamond spoke of having to "live down" the early "teenybopper" part of his career. At the same time, Neil correctly pointed out, "You see, I've never been made by publicity because I've never had it. The only publicity I've ever had was the success that I had."

Despite any digs coming from the hip side of the world, *Serenade* became yet another significant commercial success, rising to #5 on the *Billboard* top two hundred and yielding two hit singles. "I've Been This Way Before" would make it into the top forty, but it was an even more poetic, catchy, and seductive number called "Longfellow Serenade" that would rise far higher, reaching #5 in October of 1974. A third single from the *Serenade* album, the reggae-tinged "The Last Picasso," did not hit the charts with any force, but was another standout in the relatively arty context of *Serenade*.

As Diamond once explained it to me, "Longfellow Serenade" was written as a romantic song about a man wooing a woman with poetry. Still, I for one have always believed in my heart of hearts that the double-entendre in using the name of Henry Wadsworth Longfellow here had to be intentionally suggestive, though I may simply be erecting some strange fantasy. In any case, "Longfellow Serenade" also included a prominent reference to "winged flight" that sounded far more carnal than any journey Jonathan Livingston Seagull might have taken.

True to his earlier word to spend more time at home, Diamond did not hit the road in support of *Serenade*. Instead, as his working sabbatical continued, he began to write and record what would ultimately be the finest and most lived-in album of his entire career, at least to date— a deeply felt personal album that he called *Beautiful Noise*.

In an initially surprising but ultimately savvy move, Diamond chose this time to shake things up by asking his Malibu neighbor Robbie Robertson, well regarded as the lead guitarist, main songwriter, and producer of the Band, to produce his next studio album. To the self-consciously groovy rock press of the period, the very notion of pop superstar Neil Diamond working with a critics' darling like Robertson seemed like a shock to the system, the formation of a genuine rock-and-roll odd couple. As Robertson would later tell VH1, he was not bothered in the least: "A lot of people, they were like, 'Wait a minute is this a put on? What's going on here? This doesn't fit musically. You. Neil Diamond. Your background. His background. And I felt like, don't you tell *me* what fits. I'll *show* you what fits. And we made a record that I'm very, very proud of. It was probably his best received record ever." *Beautiful Noise*, the album that Diamond and Robertson made together, with the latter's producer credit unusually appearing right on the front cover, would eventually herald Diamond's full return to the music world, bringing the singer back to the stage at last from his self-imposed exile.

The initial spark for this conceptual album was Diamond's interest in drawing upon a sometimes painful but extremely important period in his own life. As Neil explained, "I thought that I'd like to try somehow to tell the story of what it was like in Tin Pan Alley with all the other aspiring young writers. Some of them huge successes, most of us knocking around on the streets and hoping for a break."

With the help of Robertson, who first achieved some fame backing up Bob Dylan, Diamond was going to turn through his own back pages with electrifying results.

Rolling Stone's Ben Fong-Torres was there at the Kendrum studios in Burbank with Diamond and Robertson during the completion of the *Beautiful Noise* album, reporting for his cover story on Diamond, a man whom he memorably concluded was, when not "fencing with the world . . . just a nice Jewish *mensch*."

Fong-Torres's piece for the magazine captured the convivial and productive mood of the two men's collaboration. As Diamond pointed out, the pair actually shared a little more common ground than others might have expected: "We really tried to cover a milieu that I spent quite a bit of time, that Robbie passed through briefly on his way to New Orleans, and we're familiar with a lot of the same characters, a lot of the same experiences, and when we first got together and started to think seriously about doing an album, we kind of groped around and one of the subjects that we covered was our shared experiences in New York."

At the same time, Diamond acknowledged that he understood full well why some were somewhat taken aback by his musical pairing with the Band leader. "We thought it was an odd combination too," Diamond confessed. "Robbie being so rooted in his thing and me being in my area. But we thought the combination of the two would create a third thing that neither of us had experienced."

In that same piece, Diamond made it clear that he wasn't working with Robertson in some desperate bid for hipness by association. Indeed, one comment from Diamond was a charming put-down of the very concept of hipness itself. "Hip was something frivolous people had time to be," he said. "I didn't have time to be hip and with it and groovy. I was dealing with something that was much more important with my life and trying to write songs that had substance. And hip is bullshit. It doesn't cut deep. It cuts for today and tomorrow."

Both in Ben Fong-Torres's 1976 *Rolling Stone* cover story on Diamond and in my own interview more than a decade later, it became clear that a mutual admiration society of sorts had formed between him and Robertson, two talented singer-songwriters from slightly different worlds. "I thought his early stuff was fantastic," Robertson told me in *Rolling Stone* more than a decade later. "He thought up these melodies that you couldn't get out of your head. And sometimes it was aggravating that you couldn't get one of those songs to go away, but that just proved how infectious they really were."

As Robertson saw it, Neil Diamond had a singular place in the musical universe, with a huge and devoted following that could not get enough of him. "My theory is that there was a musical vacuum out there between Elvis Presley and Frank Sinatra," Robertson explained. "And there was this huge audience that said, 'We've got to have something,' and they adopted Neil. And when you go to see him, it's like 'What is going on here?' These people are *hypnotized*. He can probably sell more seats than Bruce Springsteen, you know. And it's not because it's the hip thing to do; it's because there's an audience there that needs this fix."

In Robertson, meanwhile, Diamond had found a producer who demanded and helped draw out the very best in him, and that's exactly what he got on *Beautiful Noise*. The overall concept of the album served to effectively ground Diamond's writing, and he retraced his own steps here with great feeling and artistry. For Neil, music had always been a highly personal matter, and the more personal it got, the better it tended to sound. *Beautiful Noise* was a homey masterpiece or, as he wrote in his own brief liner notes essay for the album, "a series of recollections seen through the eyes of a young songwriter."

It was Neil's firstborn daughter, Marjorie, who would give the album its title. Diamond was staying in his usual suite at the Sherry Netherlands Hotel on Fifth Avenue with his two daughters, Marjorie and Elyn, when one afternoon, the sounds of the Puerto Rican Day Parade filled the rooms. The girls were coloring with their father when Marjorie looked up and said, "What a beautiful noise, Dad."

Neil has always recognized a memorable title when he heard one, and he instinctively knew that "beautiful noise" might work as a song for the new album that he had started with Robbie Robertson, reflecting his own time in Tin Pan Alley. That evening, with his girls and his parents there, Diamond turned on a tape recorder and started the song. Part of the family demo can be heard on *In My Lifetime*. As Diamond explained in the liner notes of that collection, "It was the first song written for the *Beautiful Noise* album and really put us on the right track for the story we wanted to tell.

Beautiful Noise is full of great, evocative songs, and in "If You Know What I Mean" he had written his finest so far during his time with Columbia. The track, which peaked at #11, is a song of considerable depth with a certain winning mystery. The same could be said of "Dry Your Eyes," a slow-burning song informed by a sense of his own generation's loss of innocence. It was "Dry Your Eyes" that Diamond would ultimately perform during his convincing if odd-man-out performance with the Band at The Last Waltz concert, for which he wore a light blue suit, red shirt, and sunglasses at night.

"Dry Your Eyes" was an especially fitting choice to play with the Band since after years of writing alone, Diamond had cowritten this fine song with Robertson. Diamond's performance was quite strong by any standard. Still, by the all-star group's finale version of Bob Dylan's "I Shall Be Released," Neil Diamond, standing next to Joni Mitchell with Neil Young on her other side, started to move farther from the center of the stage, and as the song ended, he appeared to be the first to leave the stage. Later he would say that he had flown back and forth from Los Angeles to San Francisco that day, so that he could have Thanksgiving dinner with his family and put his kids to bed.

Neil told me that backstage he had warned Bob Dylan that he had better be good because the audience was *his*. Unsurprisingly, Dylan seemed slightly taken aback by the warning, then went out and made the crowd his own. Watching Scorsese's brilliant film of The Last Waltz concert again recently, I was struck by the fact that judging Neil Diamond harshly for the crime of not being Bob Dylan, or even Neil Young, makes a lot less sense than embracing him because he's the very best Neil Diamond we've got.

If The Last Waltz did not find Diamond in his natural environment, his 1977 live album *Love at the Greek* certainly did, documenting his big return to the road. "I came back with a new enthusiasm toward writing and recording and also toward performing," Diamond said. "And I think I was a different and a better performer when I came back. It seemed like I grew up somewhat in those four years."

Part of this growth was a noticeable change in style. Just as punk and disco styles were beginning to emerge, Diamond seemed to dress for success in his own way. In the angry era of punk, Neil's polished and shimmering shirts were easy targets. When asked about those shirts, he made no apologies whatsoever. "I've worn these glass beaded shirts for years because it makes it a little bit easier for people to see me," he said. "And a little of me is a contrarian, and if somebody says, you know, I really *hate* those shirts, I'm going to order another dozen of those shirts."

Increasingly, Diamond was accused of seeming more like a Las Vegas showman than a rock-and-roll star, despite the fact that he had never played Sin City. Then, in the summer of 1976, Diamond made his high-profile Vegas debut by opening the Aladdin Theatre for the Performing Arts. Diamond won big here once again, despite an oddly timed and mysteriously motivated attempted drug bust at his home the night before he was planning to fly to Vegas. Reportedly, the L.A. police had been tipped by some obvious nonfan that Diamond was in possession of a stash of cocaine. Perhaps fearing gun violence or worse from the man who sang "Song Sung Blue," a reported fifty members of the L.A. police and sheriff's department descended on Diamond's Holmby Hills home, not far from the Playboy Mansion. In the end, the authorities found less than a single ounce of marijuana and nothing else in his residence, and no arrest was made. Though even a tiny amount of marijuana might have been considered embarrassing coming from the man who wrote "The Pot Smoker's Song," Diamond somehow rallied himself and went to Las Vegas the next day as scheduled. The day of his big debut, he received word that he was being charged with a misdemeanor for possession of marijuana. The charge was later dropped after Neil agreed to a drug awareness course.

A drug bust, even one that turned out to be pretty much a bust itself, didn't overnight make Diamond much more hip to some. "I don't think being hip has played any real, meaningful part in my career because it hasn't affected what I write," Neil said.

Still, Diamond's live show was getting bigger, bolder, and more full of hits. His band, always top-notch, expanded further to fit the demand,

and now grew bigger and better as well with the addition of new members like King Errisson on percussion, Tom Hensley on piano, and Doug Rhone on guitar, while Reine Press's wife, Linda, was a new presence as Diamond's backing vocalist.

Increasingly, Diamond was carving out his own musical niche, and a big one at that.

Peter Asher, the former member of Peter & Gordon who went on to be a highly successful producer and manager, was working with Diamond in 2000 when I asked him for *Behind the Music* how Diamond was viewed. "I think the fact that Neil's fan base is so huge and so committed and so devoted is also why he becomes the butt of other people's humor. In the music community, he was always held with tremendous respect."

In that same show, Paul Shaffer still seemed amazed that anyone would put down Neil Diamond for his big show and increasingly flashy performance style. "It's show business," he said. "Rock & roll is about pizzazz and show business and selling, selling a song. Didn't Jerry Lee Lewis get on top of his piano? He can't play the piano from up there. What was he doing up there? Showmanship. Come on, it's part of rock & roll."

Shaffer was right, yet by the end of the seventies, even following *Beautiful Noise*, Diamond seemed to draw further from the rock world. And the trajectory of his career only seemed to apply to one man.

1977's *Love at the Greek*, a double live album recorded at the same venue he had helped make even more famous with *Hot August Night*, documented another of Diamond's big homecomings. Indeed, this time everything seemed bigger—not just the band, but also the audience. This time Mayor Tom Bradley was in attendance, as was the up-and-coming Olivia Newton John. Diamond asked "I Am Woman" singer Helen Reddy and actor Henry Winkler to sing along with him on "Song Sung Blue," the latter even gamely accommodating Neil's request that he do so in character as the Fonz from *Happy Days*. For his part, Diamond appeared happy to share the spotlight with these guest stars, warmly calling them "*bubby*" and "*bubula*." Such blatant examples of open-air uses of Yiddish slang did not hurt the album's chart performance, as the double live album rose into the top ten.

Diamond was now a multimedia star. In addition to the *Love at the Greek* album, also produced by Robbie Robertson, that also went top ten, there was the *Neil Diamond: Love at the Greek* television special produced by Gary Smith and Dwight Hemion. The show would be nominated for four Emmy awards.

For his next album, 1977's *I'm Glad You're Here with Me Tonight*, Diamond would turn to a new producer with a musical past closer to his own than Robbie Robertson. Bob Gaudio had become famous as a key member, writer, and producer of Frankie Valli and the Four Seasons. Even earlier, the Bronx-born, New Jersey–raised Gaudio had hit it big at fifteen by cowriting "Short Shorts" for his group, the Royal Teens. Years later, Gaudio would be instrumental in putting together *Jersey Boys*, the Tony-winning Broadway musical history of Frankie Valli and the Four Seasons.

Like Diamond, Gaudio was a man of considerable musical range, and had a true knack for what made a pop song work. The album also saw Diamond further loosening up when it came to songwriting. Having cowritten "Dry Your Eyes" with Robertson, Diamond seemed to enter an increasingly collaborative period in his musical career. *I'm Glad You're Here with Me Tonight* reflected this, For instance, it was Gaudio and wife Judy Parker who wrote the album's romantic title track, not Diamond. The album also featured covers of Joni Mitchell's "Free Man in Paris" and the Beach Boys' masterpiece "God Only

Knows," written by the great Brian Wilson and Tony Asher, the latter becoming a number-one adult contemporary radio hit.

The *I'm Glad You're Here with Me Tonight* album, which shared its title with another Emmy-nominated Diamond TV special, would perform well on the charts, hitting #6 on the *Billboard* album chart. The biggest single from the album at the time was "Desiree,'" a lusty tale of sexual innocence lost that had a pulse all its own and went to #16 on the pop charts. "To me it's a song with a great groove, a cooking record," Diamond said. Neil also revealed that he had written the song in his Malibu beach house "so there's definitely some ocean vibes going on in that one."

Ultimately, another song originally recorded for the *I'm Glad You're Here with Me Tonight* album would go on to have an extraordinary impact on Diamond's career. The genesis of "You Don't Bring Me Flowers" reflected the reality that Diamond was now a veteran superstar traveling in rarefied circles. Diamond had written the song, he once told me, because he had been seated near legendary TV writer and producer Norman Lear at comedy giant George Burns's eightieth birthday party. Diamond asked Lear what new show he was working on that needed a new theme, and Lear told him about *All That Glitters*, a new project about traditional male and female roles being reversed. When Diamond suggested that he write a torch song sung by a man, Lear asked if Diamond would work on it with noted songwriters Marilyn and Alan Bergman, and he was happy to accommodate. In the end, the brief song that the three wrote at the piano wasn't used on Lear's short-lived sitcom but instead expanded and put on Diamond's latest album.

Early in 1977, Gary Guthrie, a disc jockey working for WAKY-AM in Louisville, Kentucky, made what turned out to be a most fortunate discovery. After Diamond had presented his former classmate

Barbra Streisand with an Academy Award for "Evergreen" from *A Star Is Born* (a movie for which Diamond had perhaps prematurely passed on costarring), she had recorded her own version of "You Don't Bring Me Flowers." Guthrie took the two versions and played them at the same time on two different turntables, and found himself taken aback by how well Diamond's distinguished baritone seemed to blend with Streisand's singular soprano. Soon Guthrie spliced together, in effect, his own "duet" of the song that he started playing on the air.

Neil Diamond was a busy man at the time. Beyond all the music he was making, on Valentine's Day in 1978 his wife, Marcia, gave birth to their second son, Micah Joseph Diamond. Having learned his lesson, Diamond took time off from performing to be closer to home this time. But by the same token, he was not a man to look an obvious smash hit gift in the mouth. Inspired by the success of their fake duet, the pair of recovering Erasmus High students met at Cherokee Studios in Hollywood and recorded an actual duet version produced by Bob Gaudio. It went all the way to #1 on the pop charts in November 1978, Diamond's first song to hit the very top of the charts since "Song Sung Blue" five years earlier.

The success of the duet version of "You Don't Bring Me Flowers" was so massive and instantaneous that Diamond's plan to record an ambitious double-album set of cover songs and originals to be called *The American Popular Song* was cut short in order to put out an album called *You Don't Bring Me Flowers,* featuring the smash duet, that quickly reached the top five itself.

Diamond arguably paid a price for such mainstream success. The media increasingly dealt with Diamond less as musical force and more as a commercial and cultural phenomenon, and not always positively. Reviewing the *You Don't Bring Me Flowers* album in *Rolling Stone,* for instance, critic Stephen Holden began this way: "Like Sylvester Stallone, Neil Diamond is an icon of the American Dream, wearing his street-toughened ego as a badge of artistic authenticity. No other pop singer capitalizes quite so heavily on the naked celebration of having Made It. If Diamond seemed garishly out of place in Martin Scorsese's *The Last Waltz*, the mere fact of his presence was a testament to his indomitable will to conquer."

However the press viewed Diamond now, the hits just kept coming. In addition to its title ballad, *You Don't Bring Me Flowers* also featured a more up-tempo top-twenty hit, a song he had written with his guitarist, Richard Bennett, with the evocative and possibly provocative title "Forever in Blue Jeans."

Diamond has spoken of the important contribution Bennett's guitar lick made to the song, and explained that for him the message of "Forever in Blue Jeans" was that "the simple things are really the important things." Still, such a nice sentiment did not stop the naysayers from pointing out that the Neil Diamond they easily spotted onstage was rarely in blue jeans. Such criticism seemed to come with the rich musical territory he was now seen as occupying.

Like his onetime neighbor Elvis Presley, Neil Diamond was in some ways a bigger star than ever. Diamond had already long been a genre in his own right, but now as rock music shattered in a number of directions, including punk, pop, and disco, Diamond suddenly had lots of high-profile company. Popular recording artists like Barry Manilow and Kenny Rogers had joined Diamond in this new middle of the road. This mostly mellow radio format provided a profitable port in the musical storm, but being segregated also seemed to reduce the musical range of what music was heard from them, particularly in the case of Diamond, who had always gladly covered the musical waterfront.

In 1988, I asked Neil in *Rolling Stone* if he had ever resented being lumped in with Manilow and Rogers and consigned to the middle of the road. "Not really," he said, "as long as I'm number one, you know?" In retrospect, I think I must have put that question mark at the end of Diamond's answer because I wasn't entirely certain that either one of us totally bought its semibrash sentiment.

I followed up by asking Diamond if he felt that he fit into this MOR category. "I don't," Neil answered forthrightly. "I think some of that was created around me, and they kind of came into it. But it's kind of nice to be lumped. I kind of always felt kind of lonely out there by myself."

This man who had long felt like "a male solo singer in a world of groups" now noted that he had no shortage of company. Diamond identified Elton John, whose famed American live debut at the Troubadour Neil had introduced onstage, as the first artist to join his genre. "Up until then, I was completely alone," he said. Before long there were others, and he was sharing the airwaves with major new stars like John Denver and Manilow. "For boy singers it's been pretty lonesome out there," he added. "So I'm happy to see a single guy come along and keep it happening out there while I'm resting."

Appropriately, Diamond seemed a tad less pleased when I asked what it felt like when some pop pundits dismissed him as being "slick." "Well," Neil said before taking a long pause, "when I hear 'slick,' it's like a Broadway show would be slick. Everything is like a machine; it works to perfection. And that would be pretty boring after a while. I think if I were slick, I couldn't do it for twenty years. There always has to be an unknown element. Something that makes this night different or this record different from all others. A professional, yes. Extraordinarily particular, yes . . . Hard working, intense, focused, serious, yes. Slick? . . . I don't see it."

This was one of those moments when even I realized one of the benefits of Diamond's many years focused on such an introspective form of popular art, one of the many reasons that he endured while so many others faded from the arena. All of this added up to further demonstrate that Neil Diamond continued to understand the high art and the big business of being Neil Diamond better than anybody else on earth. Even me.

As the seventies wound down, Diamond was already planning his next big move, and his first movie that would actually come to be. For his last album of the decade, 1979's *September Morn*, Diamond had struck up a significant new songwriting partnership with the French singer-songwriter and entertainer Gilbert Bécaud.

Like Diamond, Bécaud was known for the charismatic live performances that earned him the nickname "Monsieur 100,000 Volts." After the French star attended one of Diamond's concerts in Paris, the two got together in Bécaud's apartment and started writing together. They came up with the highly romantic title track to *September Morn*.

At one point, however, Diamond could not decide whether to feature "September Morn" on his next album or another moving ballad that he had recently written with his longtime keyboard player, Alan Lindgren, called "Hello Again." By this time, Diamond already knew that he would need at least one big ballad for the movie in which he was planning to star. Graciously, because the movie's sound track was to come out on another label, Diamond gave Columbia their first choice of the two songs.

They chose "September Morn." Indeed, the song would become the album's title track, beating out another title he considered at the time that seemed to hint at things to come, *Songs from the Ark*. "Hello Again" would have to wait for a little something that would bring Diamond into the eighties in an even bigger way, called *The Jazz Singer*.

However, not everything was easy for Diamond in 1979. While touring, Diamond had experienced some persistent back pain and numbness in his right leg. Medical examination revealed that his spinal cord was being compressed by a tumor, thankfully a benign one. Still, he would have to undergo what *Time* magazine would later report was "a twelve-hour operation followed by three months in a wheelchair, uncertain whether he would ever walk again."

Years later, Diamond would recall this trying time during an interview with *Entertainment Tonight*. He remembered joking with his wife as he was wheeling into the recovery room at Cedars-Sinai Medical Center that if things went badly, she could just put some sequins on his wheelchair before taking him out to the stage. One can only presume that Diamond was under very serious pressure, especially because he said sequins and not glass beads.

Diamond would, of course, walk again, perform again, and even aggressively sling love again. By the end of the seventies, Neil had survived this major health scare. Now all he had to do was survive a place far more frightening—Hollywood.

Song Sung 10

AMAZED AND CONFUSED

Maybe yesterday's rhyme was for yesterday's time
And the future's not ours to see

—"YESTERDAY'S SONGS," BY NEIL DIAMOND

I DON'T LOVE THE EIGHTIES.

As decades in human history go, the eighties, at least what I recall of them, weren't so great. A combo platter of love and hate seems like a far more appropriate, and even generous, emotional response to a time that would bring our world an overabundance of things—good, bad, *and* ugly.

In no particular order, there was crack, glasnost, AIDS, Rush Limbaugh, Tiananmen Square, political correctness, compact discs, no-fault divorce, *Flashdance*, mobile phones, trickle-down economics, Smurfs, personal computers, *The Oprah Winfrey Show*, Rubik's cube, MTV, the attempted assassination of Ronald Reagan, Donkey Kong, the explosion of the space shuttle *Challenger*, aerobics, leveraged buyouts, Madonna, hair bands, the attempted assassination of Pope John Paul II, hip-hop, hostile takeovers, the Exxon *Valdez* oil spill, alternative rock, leg warmers, hardcore punk, the dismantling of the

Berlin Wall, *The Cosby Show*, megamergers, Culture Club, Donald Trump, and *Revenge of the Nerds*.

These were dramatic and trying times that inspired many of us to ask important and timeless questions, like "Who shot JR?" and "Where's the beef?"

I would argue that one of the things the eighties brought the world—good, bad, and ugly all at the same time—was a popular new brand of mass-marketed irony. This was irony in a far purer form than our systems were previously trained to process. The eighties were the decade, for example, when David Letterman's brilliantly dry late-night show arrived and made irony a popular group sport among college students and other insomniacs. This breakthrough built on the earlier groundbreaking advances of Steve Martin in the late seventies, who pushed the art of stand-up irony to new heights. By the end of the eighties, my wiseass generation had come of age with its tongue now surgically attached to its cheek.

Irony and Neil Diamond, however, have never been an easy fit. The man wrote great songs, not good *kitsch*. As a guy to hang with, Neil Diamond has, as I can personally vouch, a fine sense of irony and a fully functioning wit as well as a disarming tendency to self-deprecate. However, as a serious and undervalued popular artist, there is virtually *nothing* about Neil Diamond that is in any way ironic.

One of Diamond's finest songs ever is called "If You Know What I Mean," and in his music, Neil consistently and demonstrably *means* what he says and sings. He writes songs to express himself. He performs concerts to entertain other people. He dresses up in shiny clothes at those concerts so that folks who pay good money to see him in arenas and stadiums can actually *see* him. As an artist, Neil Diamond is to my eyes an unabashed expressionist with a bold dash of primitivism. He puts himself on the line, openly expressing a lifetime of those feelings boldly, beautifully, and intensely with no sense of ironic detachment whatsoever.

I say all of the above not to hint that Neil Diamond struggled in the eighties because of any irony deficiency on his part. Indeed, a decade and a half into his career as a musical hit maker, Diamond would start off this new decade with the single most successful studio album of his career, the smash soundtrack to *The Jazz Singer*. Neil's popularity as a live performer, meanwhile, continued to grow around the world. Even as a new generation of video icons emerged to try and kill off the radio star for good, the emotional connection that Neil Diamond shared with his following was hardly a love on the rocks.

What I'm seeking to explain, and perhaps explain away, is my own shameful, ugly truth that for a brief time in this Age of Irony, I allowed my lifelong love of Neil to enter what might best be termed a "Diamond latency period." Sigmund Freud, who never wrote about Neil Diamond, though Neil was kind enough to mention *him* in "Done Too Soon," wrote of a latency period of reduced sexuality occurring between around the age of seven and adolescence. That's *not* the latency period that I'm addressing here. Rather, I am speaking of my own passing phase of reduced public displays of affection toward Neil Diamond.

According to the best available medical records, my own short but still painful Diamond latency period began in 1978 when I fled the emotional fallout of my parent's extended divorce-a-palooza and sought temporary asylum at Loomis Chaffee, a prep school in Windsor, Connecticut. This wonderful institution gave me a great education and saved my sanity, if not my life. Musically speaking, though, I soon discovered that I had now entered enemy territory. There I was in all my pudgy glory, a stocky, pasty Jew in New Wave clothes whose holy triumvirate of great tunes was Bob Dylan, Neil Diamond, and Elvis Costello, entering a new world where music began and ended with the stony ramblings of the Grateful Dead.

Yes, I still loved and listened to Neil Diamond, but increasingly my quality time with Neil's records took place on the down low, on headphones rather than blasting in the dorms with my door wide open.

In retrospect, I believe that I hid my love for Neil from the world for a good part of the late seventies and eighties because, as an approval-seeking adolescent, I was worried that there might be some stigma associated with being a teenage Diamondhead. This might have been unforgivable, but it was also understandable. To openly worship Diamond in those circles did not make one more hip by association, and as a teen, what could be more crucial than the fine art of being cool?

When I first sought exile at Loomis, in that same headstrong rush that saw me publicly mock the Dead, I had literally dragged a group of day students with cars to drive some of us to go see the opening of Woody Allen's latest masterpiece, *Manhattan,* at some movie palace near Hartford. Based on my experiences of lining up to see new Woody Allen movies in New York and New Jersey, I had insisted that we go many hours early to score tickets. I was then amazed and confused as my gang of understanding new friends sat virtually alone in the empty theater, watching this masterpiece in a preppy sort of isolation. It was then that I realized the harsh lesson that despite what growing up in my neck of New Jersey might have suggested, the world was, in fact, *not* Jewish.

So when *The Jazz Singer* came out in the winter of 1980, I snuck out and saw it alone in Times Square during vacation, while the rest of the guys in my dorm were probably off somewhere playing lacrosse or getting stoned while listening to the Dead's *American Beauty*. And as far as I can tell, I never wrote a word about Neil in the *Loomis Chaffee Log*, though I came in second place in some *Hartford Courant* high school journalism competition for my deeply personal piece defending Bob Dylan's born-again Christian music. I consider this failure to stand up for what I loved to be just another shameful part of my temporary Neil Diamond fan witness relocation program.

The beginning of the end of my Diamond latency period came a few years later while studying at Cornell. It's often darkest before the dawn, and I hit my personal bottom in 1982. I am now ashamed to say I have absolutely no memory of the release of Neil's album *On the Way to the Sky*—a total Diamond blackout. Then one afternoon, I *knew* I had to make a change. I was in my off-campus apartment in Ithaca, New York, hanging up a poster of my latest musical hero, Prince, that came in his *Controversy* album: a poster that featured the Purple One striking an odd pose in a bizarre sort of funky G-string. Suddenly it hit me. If I could put a picture of Prince in a pasty up on my bedroom wall, then I could damn well let my freak flag fly and play Neil Diamond, loudly and proudly.

And so, embracing a part of myself that had been denied for far too long, I pulled out my copy of *The Jazz Singer* sound track from my closet, opened my door and windows wide, and let the transcendent beauty "America" ring out for all to hear. I listened to his words about being "in the eye of the storm" and feeling "freedom's light burning warm." Four minutes and eighteen seconds later, I had not simply reclaimed a part of my soul, I had done something far more important. I had made the long journey not to "America," but back to my truest self.

In a flash, I had learned to stop worrying and love Neil Diamond. Despite years of movie offers, planned film projects, and one failed yet ultimately profitable screen test, Neil Diamond still somehow remained a Hollywood virgin of sorts, until he walked onto the set of *The Jazz Singer* for the very first day of shooting on January 8, 1980, in Maricopa, California. After years of pursuing acting with various degrees of seriousness, Neil had at long last finally agreed to make his move, and he did so in a very big and ambitious way, by both starring and writing music in a remake of *The Jazz Singer.* "Sometimes you have to risk it all," read one of the lines on the poster of the movie, but those same words could just as easily have applied to Diamond as they did to Jess Robin, the character he played in the film.

In some broad ways, the movie *would* mirror Diamond's own life: the story of a Jewish kid from New York who leaves everything behind to pursue his dream of making popular music in Los Angeles. "It's the story of someone who wants to break away from the traditional family situation and find his own path," Neil told me for *Behind the Music.* "And in that sense, it *is* my story."

Still, despite this sort of typecasting, the challenge Neil was now taking on was exponentially greater than his first and only other role as an actor: playing himself in a 1967 episode of *Mannix* called "The Many Deaths of Saint Christopher." First, there was the built-in risk that came with attempting to remake a film classic. The original version of *The Jazz Singer,* starring Al Jolson, had come out in 1927 and made history as the first full-length motion picture with synchronized dialogue. Diamond's *Jazz Singer* wasn't even the first remake. There was a 1952 film version starring Danny Thomas, as well as a 1959 TV adaptation starring Jerry Lewis.

For all that proven cinematic history, the idea of featuring the Jewish experience so prominently seemed in and of itself risky in a year when the ten top-grossing films would include such relatively less Semitic fare as *The Blue Lagoon, Airplane!, Any Which Way You Can, Urban Cowboy,* and *The Empire Strikes Back*, none of which prominently featured the Yiddish language nearly as much as *The Jazz Singer.*

For Neil Diamond, *The Jazz Singer* experience would prove to be extremely rewarding and trying—the best of times, the worst of times. The best of times came in the form of a smash soundtrack that included three of the most popular songs of Diamond's life in music. The worst of times came from the realization that a solitary man like Diamond found it difficult to feel at home in a creative realm where so much control had to be shared by so many.

Still, as Neil told me for his *Behind the Music* episode in 2000, "I felt it was time for me to try something on film that would give me a real chance to see if I had any acting chops, and also more importantly would give me the chance to write some music."

The music Diamond created for *The Jazz Singer*, with Bob Gaudio as his producer once again, was eclectic even by his own standards, from the personal and patriotic "America" to traditional Jewish music like "Adon Olom" to big ballads like "Hello Again" and "Love on the Rocks" to infectious power pop like "You Baby" to harder-edged rock like "Amazed and Confused" to "On the Robert E. Lee," which sounded as if it could have come from some lost MGM musical.

For the *Jazz Singer* sound track, Diamond collaborated on five songs with Gilbert Bécaud, including "Love on the Rocks," which had started as a reggae-tinged tune called "Scotch on the Rocks." As Neil explained in the liner notes for *In My Lifetime*, scotch on the rocks was his French friend's drink of choice, and initially they considered the song a bit of a lark. "When the verse was formed, Gilbert and I felt the song had more serious possibilities and so we tried it as a straight two-and-four ballad," Neil said.

Diamond's band, which now included ace percussionist Vince Charles, was also featured prominently on the album, with Linda Press credited along with Gaudio for the album's vocal arrangements. Band members also increasingly featured as Neil's songwriting partners, with Lindgren cowriting the music for "Hello Again," Richard Bennett cowriting the music for "Amazed and Confused," and Doug Rhone for "Acapulco."

The triumph of *The Jazz Singer*, however, would not come easily for Diamond. Even by the standards of Hollywood, *The Jazz Singer* would prove a difficult shoot. The original director on the film, Sidney J. Furie, who had previously helmed *Lady Sings the Blues* starring Diana Ross, was replaced during filming by Richard Fleisher, whose previous big screen musical effort was *Doctor Doolittle*. Neil's original leading lady, Deborah Raffin, was also let go early in the production and replaced by Lucie Arnaz. Then there was the fact that a movie newcomer like Diamond would have to prove himself worthy of acting alongside the likes of one of the most acclaimed actors of all time, Laurence Olivier. Remarkably, to my eyes and possibly my eyes only, Diamond would at the very least hold his own with a pleasantly nuanced performance alongside the more theatrical work of Olivier.

Before filming began, Diamond ran into Dustin Hoffman, Olivier's *Marathon Man* costar, and confessed just how frightened he was about acting with this living legend. Wisely, Hoffman, who by now had actually played the part of Lenny Bruce that Neil had once sought, offered Neil some sage, actor-to-actor advice: Neil should embrace those scared feelings and put them straight into the work.

Diamond and Olivier would strike up a friendship on the set. Yet, there were still many times while making *The Jazz Singer* when Neil felt justifiably like "a fish out of water." As he recalled the expe-

rience to me in 2000, "I'd come home at night exhausted, just men-
tally exhausted . . . After the first few weeks, you know, I didn't think
I could handle it anymore. Olivier would come home after a day's
work on the set, swim laps in the hotel swimming pool and go out
with friends for dinner. I came home and fell into bed exhausted
knowing that I'd have to get up at four the next morning to study my
lines for the day."

"I really think that Neil was just a regular guy scared to death to be
acting in his first film," said Lucie Arnaz.

No matter how hard he worked through that fear, Diamond
could not compensate for the fact that, unlike the life he knew in a
recording studio, there was only so much control he could have on a
movie set. As Bob Gaudio put it, "I think that was very difficult for
him to deal with, especially because he's used to saying when things
will happen."

New difficulties arrived when the reviews for *The Jazz Singer* hit in
late 1980 and became a real critical drubbing. "My performance,
Olivier's performance, anyone who was in the film or came near it was
savaged," Neil recalled twenty years after the fact. "But it was totally ir-
relevant to me," he added. "The album, thank goodness, was accepted
and brought some of my better songs to the public."

Or as Lucie Arnaz memorably put it, "So P.S., the movie goes in
the toilet, the album makes bazillions of platinum money and I get
nothing." That said, Arnaz felt strongly, and correctly, that her world-
famous costar had been too harshly judged. "They crucified him so
bad," Arnaz said ruefully. "I think he could have been a very good
actor had the critics been a little more kind to him in his first film."

It says something that on the box for a 2002 DVD reissue of *The
Jazz Singer* the only blurb lines come from syndicated columnist
Shirley Eder, who declares, "Neil's movie is a gem," and Christopher

Sharp of *Women's Wear Daily*, who suggests, "You'll want to see it a second time."

The Jazz Singer became a box-office disappointment, though Neil Diamond fans would later make the movie dramatically more successful in the new home video format as the box-office letdown became an early hit on videocassette. And in a pattern now familiar from *Jonathan Livingston Seagull*, the big letdown of the film's reception would be balanced by the stunning success of its soundtrack, initially released not by Columbia but Capitol, because of the movie being produced by EMI Films.

The Jazz Singer soundtrack itself rose to #3 and ultimately outsold even *Jonathan Livingston Seagull*, helped no doubt by the movie's higher profile and three sizable pop hits that remain radio staples to this day. First, "Love on the Rocks" went to #2 on the pop charts in early 1981, blocked only by Lionel Richie's "Lady," while also reaching #3 on adult contemporary. Next came "Hello Again," that stately, romantic Diamond gem that Columbia had in effect passed on by choosing "September Morn" instead. The single rose to #6 on pop, #3 on adult contemporary. As Neil rightly said, "When you're hot, you're hot." Then in late spring of 1981, "America" went to #8 on the pop charts and #1 on the adult contemporary charts, proving that even in Reagan's America, great patriotism and great pop were not mutually exclusive.

If *The Jazz Singer* failed to make Neil Diamond a major movie star, the soundtrack album going multiplatinum clearly reinforced Diamond's status in the music business. This latest demonstration of Diamond's commercial appeal to record buyers came at a highly opportune moment. With Capitol Records now justifiably interested in working with Neil on a more regular basis following *The Jazz Singer*, Columbia moved in and resigned their prized act to a brand new eight-album deal with a $30 million guarantee.

Yet for all the promise of such a big deal, forces would now combine to make the remainder of the decade a relatively bumpy one in Neil Diamond's recording career. First, the industry itself was growing larger, more corporate, and less given to allowing even established artists to freely follow their own creative instincts. Then there was the reality that, like many of us, Neil Diamond was growing older each year, gradually separating him from the youngest music fans, who tended to drive hit songs. Finally, with music's new video age just about to dawn, popular music itself was poised to take an extended dip in the shallow pool, relatively speaking.

Diamond's next album, 1981's *On the Way to the Sky*, was the first hint of some of the growing tension at work. The album's biggest and best remembered hit, "Yesterday's Songs," hit #11 on the *Billboard* pop charts, yet at the same time the song sounded somewhat defeated, a very comfortable, tuneful nostalgia trip down the middle of the road. Reviewing the song in the *Los Angeles Times*, Paul Grein was harsh but not entirely wrong when he wrote that the song was "wallpaper music that's easily the least substantial single in Diamond's fifteen-year career."

According to Diamond, "Yesterday's Song" was written in the early eighties "when I guess I doubted that any of my early songs would be remembered." Ironically, as he went on to point out, that same concern would be calmed considerably when the British reggae band UB40 made "Red, Red Wine" an international hit in 1984, followed years later by the Urge Overkill hit remake of "Girl, You'll Be a Woman Soon" and many other well-earned revivals of his past catalog.

Still, *On the Way to the Sky*, which Diamond produced with his longtime drummer, Dennis St. John, as a coproducer, felt slightly overcooked on songs like the string-laden title track that hit #27. Nor could it be considered a good sign that St. John, who had been around since Diamond's Uni days, left the project and the band during the recording of the album. St. John would soon be replaced in the NDRRT—the Neil Diamond Road Racing Team, as the band would become known—by one of the *other* King's men, Elvis Presley's former drummer, Ron Tutt.

Amid the shiny surfaces of *On the Way to the Sky*, there were at least two extremely intriguing songs. "Be Mine Tonight," which sounded like some long-lost Bang hit, scraped its way into the top forty in the summer of 1982, but the track deserved far better. Emphatically less commercial but entirely fascinating was the song "Fear of the Marketplace," which seemed wonderfully out of left field on the album and perhaps hinted at Diamond's own growing issues with the fast-changing musical marketplace.

Nineteen eighty-two saw the release of the effective stopgap *12 Greatest Hits Vol. II* from Columbia, then later in the year Diamond would deliver a freshly minted smash in the unlikely form of "Heartlight." Like the rest of the world, Neil had gone to see Steven Spielberg's *E.T.* and been tremendously moved by the experience. Unlike the rest of us, however, Neil had attended the screening with songwriters Carole Bayer Sager and Burt Bacharach, both of whom had also come a long way from Tin Pan Alley. After the movie, Diamond went to Bacharach and Sager's apartment and came up with what he's called "a simple musical statement that we all felt very sincerely."

Soon they were hardly the only ones feeling "Heartlight," which became a top-five pop hit and served as the title track of Diamond's next top-ten album. *Heartlight* featured other collaborations with

Sager and Bacharach as writers and producers, and one gripping pop rocker called "I'm Alive" that Diamond cowrote with keyboard whiz David Foster. "I'm Alive" was inspired by the "sense of dread" Neil felt while driving with Bacharach back and forth to Ocean Way Recording Studios on Sunset Boulevard. That sense of dread worked out fairly well, with the single hitting #35 in February of 1983.

For the record, Neil Diamond now seemed to be getting a lot of inspiration at the movies in 1982. Seeing posters for the upcoming Warren Beatty film *Heaven Can Wait*, Diamond also wrote a lovely ballad by the same title and sent it off to Beatty. Apparently his offer of musical help arrived too late, and "Heaven Can Wait" would have to wait until Diamond included it on *In My Lifetime* in 1996.

Diamond's next studio album would have its own well-publicized troubles getting to the marketplace. As a sign of the times, Columbia Records rejected Diamond's first submitted version of an album called *Primitive*, and legal and artistic wrangling ensued, delaying the release. In the interim, Columbia issued *Classics: The Early Years*, a too short but sweet and strong retrospective of Neil's Bang days that reflected the fact that Neil had now reclaimed control of his earliest hits.

The public would finally get to hear a version of *Primitive* in 1984, but despite the smiling photo of Neil on the front cover, it was hard to imagine that Diamond was happy to find so many creative cooks in the kitchen for this A&R (artists and repertoire) process. A number of songs were removed from Diamond's original song list for the album, including one called "Hit Man" and another titled "Act Like a Man." In the end, the strongest tracks on the *Primitive* album were three outstanding songs that Diamond had written by himself: the fast-moving "Fire on the Tracks," the theatrical and nicely nostalgic "Brooklyn on a Saturday Night," and "You Make It Feel Like Christmas"—not the last song Diamond would sing with the word "Christmas" in the title, but easily the most romantic.

For all the newfound record label input, the commercial results for *Primitive* were less than pleasing for everyone concerned. The album peaked at only #35, while only the lush ballad "Turn Around" broke out of the adult contemporary ghetto at all, reaching #62 on the *Billboard* hot one hundred.

For all that, Neil Diamond's standing as a live performer only seemed to improve with every year in the eighties and the NDRRT increasingly became a family of sorts. "I never felt that Neil was a boss," his former guitarist Richard Bennett told *Behind the Music* in 2000. By this time, Bennett had enjoyed success as a producer in Nashville, but he made it clear, "I always felt that I worked *with* Neil, and I think that's part of the reason why he's kept a band—some of them for thirty years now."

"They've been with me in the trenches," Diamond told me of his band in the show. "I have a very deep sense of loyalty to them, not only as musicians, but as people. And I think that's why we've been together for so long."

Bassist Reine Press explained to me that Neil had always gone to great lengths to try and insulate his bandmates from the insanity of the road, thus creating a nurturing world of their own that they came to affectionately call "Diamondville." Reine and his backing vocalist wife, Linda, explained that they had even raised a child in Diamondville. Their daughter, Daisy, appeared herself on the *Behind the Music* episode, to explain how she came to be raised on the road.

Speaking of her parents, Daisy Press said, "The legend is that they went up to Neil and said, "Neil, what do we *do*? We're going to have this child. The road is really no place to raise a child. And he said, "No, it's *not* really but . . . we'll *make* it one, so bring her along." And so they did. "She gave a lot to this group—just having a little girl in the front of the bus," Neil said to me of Daisy. "Most of us had left our children at home. So Daisy became *our* child."

As things turned out, Neil would call upon the support of his real and surrogate family when his beloved father, Kieve, died while he was on tour in the spring of 1985.

As Neil recalled for *Behind the Music*, he received the heartbreaking news soon after walking off stage. "I got a call from my wife after I'd done a show," he told me. "And she said, 'Honey, it's not good news. Your dad passed away earlier today.'"

Neil shut down his tour to mourn his father at home, then returned to his second home on the road, now joined by a very special guest. Neil and Marcia's son, Jesse, offered to come with his father, supporting him onstage and off. "I said, Jess, as long as I can turn around, look at you, and get a smile, I'll get through the show. And he was there for me, which I'll always be thankful for."

As he had done so many times before, Diamond poured his feelings into a new set of songs he started to compose. The result was an album that he envisioned calling *The Story of My Life*. Understandably, *The Story of My Life* reflected the loss of his father very directly, especially in a powerful song he called "Angel Above My Head." Other titles for the planned album included "Falling," another excellent collaboration with Gilbert Bécaud, and a song called "Long Nights." In the liner notes to *In My Lifetime*, Neil explained that *The Story of My Life* was "an album that Columbia wasn't in love with, so eventually I scrapped it and waited for the next inspiration to come."

Only the song "The Story of My Life" from that album would emerge on Diamond's next album, 1986's optimistically titled *Headed for the Future*. Far less personal an album than it might have been, *Headed for the Future* found Diamond doing his best to try and squeeze into the MTV age. The album featured a solid new song written by Bryan Adams and then songwriting partner Jim Valance called "It Should Have Been Me." Included were songwriting collaborations between Diamond and everyone from Bacharach and Sager to Stevie Wonder ("Lost in Hollywood") to his two keyboard players, Tom Hensley and Alan Lindgren, who cowrote and coproduced the album's new title track. Earth, Wind & Fire's Maurice Starr, Burt Bacharach and Carol Bayer Sager, David Foster, Stevie Wonder, and Diamond himself were all credited as producers on assorted tracks.

The synth-laden "Headed for the Future" would put Diamond on MTV in a space-age video that was very much of its era, and even hit #10 on the adult contemporary chart, while stopping short of top forty at #53 on the pop chart. Still, the reception for *Headed for the Future* was an improvement on *Primitive*, with the album hitting a significantly more impressive #20 on the top two hundred.

Wherever Neil Diamond exactly fit into the new and not necessarily improved musical universe at the tail end of the eighties, he still commanded respect on any stage in the world that he graced. His popularity as a live entertainer was demonstrated yet again on 1987's *Hot August Night II*, his latest live album to be recorded at the Greek Theatre. As far as sequels to past classics go, *Hot August Night II* may not have exactly been *The Godfather: Part II*, but it was still an excellent keepsake that showed Diamond was as much a crowd pleaser in concert as ever. It had a fine set of songs that stretched from "Cherry, Cherry" to a convincing and suitable new rocker called "Back in L.A." that indicated that maybe now Los Angeles really did feel more and more like home to the man who wrote about being lost between two shores in "I Am . . . I Said."

It was right about this moment in the course of human events when history was made, at least for me—When David Met Neil.

To his endlessly devoted following, Neil Diamond was still at the top of the world, even if in terms of record sales and critical appreciation things had become slightly less rosy. Still, perceived hipness be damned, it was one of the thrills of my life to find myself sent by *Rolling Stone* to interview my hero, our hero, in his natural habitat in Los Angeles. Since I still didn't drive at this point, I remember walking a mile or so from my hotel to Neil's plush and welcoming old office on Melrose Place. I was met there by Neil's endlessly pleasant and helpful assistant, Alison Zanetos, who serves him well even now. Then over two easy and entertaining afternoons, I got to know the man for whom I had so many questions, all of which I happily asked and he politely answered.

The second day, I mentioned to Neil how much my mother had always loved him, a conversation-filler that would pay huge dividends for her and me soon enough.

Not long after we first met, Neil's publicist sent me two advance copies of Neil's next studio album, one copy for me and one for my mother too. *The Best Years of Our Lives*, Neil's last new album of the eighties, was far and away his best piece of work in years, easily his most appealing set of songs since *The Jazz Singer*. On this album he produced with David Foster, it finally felt like Diamond had regained his creative bearings and been allowed to once again start doing what he did better than anyone: be Neil Diamond.

The Best Years of Our Lives kicked off with a rousing title track written by Neil that suggested what it would sound like if Bruce Springsteen's E Street Band backed him. The next song was a pretty track called "Hard Time for Lovers," and listening to it, it wasn't hard to make the leap that the times of which he now sang had also been relatively hard times for an unironic, dedicated, and serious singer-songwriter such as Diamond.

Fortunately for Neil Diamond, and for those of us who love him, there would be good and even great times still ahead.

Song Sung 11

GOLD DON'T RUST

Hey boy, you look like a million.

Hey, now, show 'em what you got.

Hey boy, what you got to run from?

I'll teach you all that I forgot.

—"IN MY LIFETIME," BY NEIL DIAMOND

WHEN I FIRST ARRIVED IN LOS ANGELES IN THE SPRING OF 1991, during the late stages of world domination by the not so great American hair bands, I made house calls on behalf of *Rolling Stone* to the West Coast offices of all the major label record companies. My hope in doing so was to get to know all the key players in the industry and, God willing, perhaps even hear some good new music in the process.

One of my first stops was the office of Geffen Records on Sunset Boulevard on the border of West Hollywood and Beverly Hills, just across the street from the Roxy and the Whiskey, and up the hill from Doug Weston's Troubadour where Neil Diamond had recorded his *Gold* live album. At the time, Geffen Records was the home of the biggest band in the land: Guns N' Roses. Axl Rose, Slash and company had somehow overcome an overabundance of hair product and attitude to become a powerhouse American rock band, perhaps the last of that breed, or so it seemed then.

At Geffen Records, I met Gary Gersh, one of the label's most respected A&R visionaries and a man of great taste and talent. He played some impressive music from a forthcoming solo album by Robbie Robertson, Neil Diamond's *Beautiful Noise* producer, and a track by a fine young local band called the Freewheelers. Gersh then asked me if I wanted to hear something from the upcoming major label debut of a young band from Seattle that had achieved some serious underground buzz with their independent album called *Bleach*.

The group was called Nirvana, and the song Gersh played that day would never be forgotten. That song was called "Smells Like Teen Spirit." By an accident of fate, I had become one of the first members of the outside world to hear one of the most revolutionary songs in the history of popular music. The song's hypnotically seductive core guitar riff reminded me of Boston's FM classic "More Than a Feeling," and even my less than grungy Neil Diamond–loving ears could tell that "Smells Like Teen Spirit" was something very different and very special. Alternative rock or not, the song was a stone smash.

"Wow, that's a hit," I said to Gary, in what now sounds like an absurd case of rock critic understatement. Nonetheless, Gary seemed very glad to hear the words coming out of the mouth of someone with absolutely no potential profit motive. Little did I know that when the song came out in September of 1991, "Smells Like Teen Spirit" would become not just a hit, but also one of those exceedingly rare tracks that lead to a larger changing of the guard. If you listen closely even now to "Smells Like Teen Spirit," you can hear the thrilling sound of a million Sunset Boulevard hair bands' heads exploding in a sonic blast. Then listen again and you can hear a million grungier bands being born in garages everywhere around the world.

And so just as Neil Diamond had personally witnessed roughly three decades earlier in Tin Pan Alley when the Beatles invaded, what was popular in popular music once again turned on a dime, or much more to the point—on a great song.

On September 24, 1991, Nirvana released their major label debut, an album called *Nevermind*, a game-changing musical statement that brought a young new listening world a grungy new smell of teen spirit all its own.

Less than a month earlier, at age forty-nine, Neil Diamond had released his first new album of the new decade. A beautiful and lushly romantic effort, *Lovescape* managed to satisfy the Diamondhead faithful even if it was anything but grungy, and smelled absolutely nothing like teen spirit. Indeed, *Lovescape* arguably had a scent that was decidedly more musky and middle-aged, with its songs of the triumphs and tragedies of adult love, as well as a cover of Leonard Bernstein and Stephen Sondheim's "One Hand, One Heart" from *West Side Story* and a funny, faux-reggae number of romantic mishaps called "Lonely Lady #17" that Diamond cowrote with Vince Charles.

Grunge, it wasn't.

Though they were ultimately just two guys who both wrote great songs with real hooks and a deep sense of personal involvement in their music, nobody was *ever* going to confuse Neil Diamond with Kurt Cobain. Yet already for Neil Diamond, the nineties had started off well enough. For a popular artist who typically received most of his recognition from the masses and not from the media, Diamond must have felt some measure of consolation on January 22, 1990, when he received the

Award of Merit from the American Music Awards, an honor that had previously gone to the likes of Bing Crosby, Johnny Cash, and Paul McCartney. In accepting such a grand, lifetime achievement sort of honor, Diamond earned some airtime on the show right alongside the night's other winners like then-current chart toppers Paula Abdul, Bobby Brown, New Kids on the Block, and Milli Vanilli.

Thankfully, Neil didn't try terribly hard to fit into such contemporary pop company on *Lovescape*. Well polished by a pack of proven producers including Peter Asher, Don Was, Val Garay, Humberto Gatica, and Albert Hammond, *Lovescape* offered no shortage of beautiful music to provide the soundtrack to a midlife crisis.

Standout songs on *Lovescape* included the highly dramatic and deeply moving "If There Were No Dreams," which Diamond wrote with famed French composer Michel Legrand, and "Hooked on the Memory of You," recorded with Kim Carnes of "Bette Davis Eyes." The first duet he had released since "You Don't Bring Me Flowers" became one quite by accident. "Hooked on the Memory of You" was the happy result of an unusual birth process, having been written on the piano rather than guitar. In the liner notes to *In My Lifetime,* Neil explained the song's melody was something that he had played on piano over the years, "sort of a form of piano lesson for me." The piano lesson paid off with one of his best melodies in years.

Lovescape featured further proof that Diamond's own songcraft had not deserted him. A number of the album's other highlights were collaborations between Diamond and his band members. "Wish Everything Was Alright," a strong, stripped-down midtempo number written with Hadley Hockensmith and Doug Rhone, was effectively produced by Don Was, while "All I Really Need Is You," by Diamond and his keyboard whizzes, Tom Hensley and Alan Lindgren, is a lovely ballad too few got to hear.

The commercial performance of *Lovescape* was mixed. "Hooked on the Memory of You," which should have been more widely appreciated by all those "You Don't Bring Me Flowers" fans, only got as high as #23 on the adult contemporary chart. Doing slightly better was "Don't Turn Around," a catchy Albert Hammond and Diane Warren composition that had earlier been a reggae hit for Aswad, and would later become a pop smash for Ace of Base. Diamond's "Don't Turn Around" reached #19 on the adult contemporary chart, but failed to become a sort of reverse "Red, Red Wine" crossover. The *Lovescape* album, meanwhile, hit #44, doing slightly better in England where Diamond's chart placements were now typically stronger than at home.

By the end of 1991, Neil Diamond found an effective new way to get closer to his fans by mounting a tour called Love in the Round that presented Neil right in the center of things, performing on a specially designed 360-degree stage. This tour was another smashing success, with one homey highlight being Diamond's seven consecutive sold-out nights at Los Angeles' Great Western Forum, an achievement that more than earned him a place in that venue's new Walk of Fame.

1992 saw the release of *The Greatest Hits 1966–1992*, a double album that became a smash chart-topper in England, but was a significantly slower but still steady seller in the United States. This increasingly obvious lack of relative success at home was somewhat confusing. After all, as I wrote in my *Rolling Stone* review of *The Greatest Hits 1966–1992*: "Neil Diamond is like America itself . . . Think of it: He's hugely successful, he's done a lot of amazing things over the years, and yet it remains utterly unhip to say anything remotely nice about him."

Featuring an outstanding black-and-white portrait of Diamond by George Hurrell on the cover, *The Greatest Hits 1966–1992* was a double-disc set of mainly familiar smashes, some in live recordings, with a few surprising choices, like a previously unreleased cover of "Heartbreak Hotel" as a duet with Kim Carnes and the relatively unknown *Lovescape* track "All I Really Need Is You." Most revealing were Diamond's own brief but very interesting liner notes for the album.

Among the revelations to be found by the faithful were that for Neil as a songwriter, the melody comes first, then the words. Diamond wrote that he had originally written "Solitary Man" with Bobby Darin in mind. Though he sang the hell out of "Song Sung Blue" and "Sweet Caroline," Darin never got around to working his magic on "Solitary Man" as far as I can tell. Diamond also revealed that his original title for the melody that would achieve immortality as "Brother Love's Traveling Salvation Show" was "Mo' Getta Mo," a seemingly irredeemable title that his wife, Marcia, made clear she hated.

Finally, there was a promising hint of good things to come in Diamond's parting comments. After stating that he felt the contents of *The Greatest Hits 1966–1992* "represent not only my greatest hits, but also the best of what I've been able to do musically and lyrically so far," Neil personally asked us to "stay tuned." As he explained, "The muse is alive and well and restless at all times."

Those words were followed by Diamond's signature, a personal promise that he would more than make good on in the years to come.

The Greatest Hits 1966–1992 was not the only notable Neil Diamond retrospective to be released in 1992. That same year saw MCA issue the first substantial reissue to focus on Diamond's wildly successful years with Uni. *Glory Road 1968–1972* was one of those instances in Diamond's career when the exploitation of his catalog seemed like an actual public service. Twenty years after Diamond left the label, *Glory Road* was a vivid reminder of just how musically action packed those pivotal years in Diamond's career had really been. Along with the earlier *Classics* collection, *Glory Road* offered latter-day Diamond fans a solid introduction to some of the excellent music they might have missed. Even for now-aging and increasingly decrepit Diamondheads like myself, *Glory Road* was the best sort of trip, a look back in love, not anger.

By the early nineties, Neil's past and present record companies were hardly the only ones exploiting his catalog of past hits for fun and profit. Because there could never be enough of the real Neil to go around, tribute acts that borrowed Diamond's polished but passionate act for a living started doing big business too. Fake Diamonds had been belting out Neil's songs for years, like Jay White who apparently started paying tribute to Neil in 1982 at Mr. F's Supper Club near Detroit, Michigan. He went on to become a Vegas star first in the popular *Legends* show, where Neil was one of the first living legends to be so honored, and then on his own. White reportedly impressed not only Neil, but also more impressively, his mother Rose.

But it was in the early nineties that a new tribute act from San Francisco started making Neil's beautiful noise successfully to a whole new generation of fans. No one has ever mined Diamond's gems better than the heroic outfit that dared to call itself Super Diamond, a band that promises "the Alternative Neil Diamond Experience" and delivers the goods on that promise nightly.

When we interviewed the Super Diamond front man known as Surreal Neil (real name: Randy Cordeiro) for *Behind the Music*, he explained, "Neil has a lot of followers out there—young and old. So we get some of the people who've been into Neil from the beginning and we get a lot of the people who are just now rediscovering Neil Diamond."

When I asked Neil if imitation really was the sincerest form of flattery for him, he admitted, "I guess it's flattering, and it is a little weird. But it's good. It just . . . it tells me that people are interested."

Lots of people were very interested in Diamond's last release of 1992. A decade on from *The Jazz Singer*, Diamond released *The Christmas Album*, possibly the most successful Yuletide effort by a Jew since Irving Berlin gave the world "White Christmas."

The Christmas Album reflected a long-standing tradition of such seasonal releases from major musical artists. And as the Jewish-born father of a blended family himself, who would question his motives? Well, actually, I did while I was interviewing him for *Behind the Music*. Somewhat teasingly, I inquired if it really would have been a problem for him to throw in a couple of Chanukah classics on the album too. "Well, David, the truth is it just so happens that they have *much* better songs," Neil told me with a big smile.

All that great Christmas music and Neil's massive international audience combined to make *The Christmas Album* a major hit, going platinum and reaching #8 on the *Billboard* top two hundred. Diamond's version of "Morning Has Broken," the traditional song famously reinvented by Cat Stevens in the seventies, even became an unlikely top-forty single in England. Much of *The Christmas Album* was fairly traditional, though "White Christmas" was a little more off-white thanks to an interesting doo-wop-inspired arrangement. Diamond also found room to cover John Lennon's antiwar Christmas classic, "Happy Christmas (War Is Over)" as well his own lost gem from *Primitive*, "You Make It Feel Like Christmas," giving this romantic number a fine and welcoming new home. And like an earlier version by Bruce Springsteen, Neil Diamond proved that Saint Nick could rock a little on "Santa Claus Is Coming to Town."

I, for one occasionally lapsed Jew, loved Neil's "Little Drummer Boy" and found his a capella "God Rest Ye Merry, Gentlemen" an excellent showcase for Diamond's deep and distinctive voice, whomever or whatever you happen to worship. Produced by Peter Asher, with some excellent string arrangements by Beck's father, David Campbell, *The Christmas Album* hit #8 on the *Billboard* album charts in December 1992, making it Neil's first top-ten album in America in a decade. It had not hurt one bit that Diamond promoted the album prominently on HBO with *Neil Diamond's Christmas Special,* filmed during his Love in the Round tour. As critic Adam Sandler wrote in his review of the show in *Variety*, "Neil Diamond brings the passion of hot August nights to the 12 days of Christmas."

In any known faith, such success tends to beget more of the same. And in 1994, Neil Diamond would release *The Christmas Album II.* This seasonal sequel was most notable for its reggae version of "Rudolph the Red Nosed Reindeer." Predictably, perhaps, the album was not quite the event the original had become, peaking at #51 on the *Billboard* album charts.

In between seasonal musical greetings came 1993's *Up on the Roof: Songs from the Brill Building.* Like *Beautiful Noise* before it, *Up on the Roof* was a sort of salute to Diamond's musical roots in Tin Pan Alley. But unlike *Beautiful Noise,* Diamond paid his respects here by covering some of the most notable songs of the time, from the opening "You've Lost That Lovin' Feeling" (written by Barry Mann, Cynthia Weil, and Phil Spector), recorded as a duet with Dolly Parton, to Goffin and King's "Up on the Roof," Leiber and Stoller's "Love Potion Number Nine," and his old mentors Barry and Greenwich's "Do Wah Diddy Diddy," recorded with the alternative group Mary's Danish that was managed by Peter Asher. Diamond's own composition was a version of "Ten Lonely Guys," the song he had written with nine other struggling songwriters at the time that became one of his first covers when Pat Boone sang it. Despite very mixed reviews, *Up on the Roof: Songs from the Brill Building* performed very respectably, reaching #28 on the *Billboard* two hundred.

The year 1994 was again the best of times and the worst of times for Neil Diamond.

On the positive side, a funny thing happened on Neil's way toward the middle-aged irrelevance to which certain quarters of the media seemed in a rush to consign him. Suddenly, almost out of left field, Neil found himself becoming hip again, or becoming hip the first time, depending on how you looked at it. The flashpoint for this sudden infusion of credibility was when Neil's songs started popping up in all the right places, such as very prominently on the sound track of director Quentin Tarantino's influential film smash *Pulp Fiction*. Tarantino had heard the Chicago band Urge Overkill's surprisingly faithful rendition of Diamond's Bang hit "Girl, You'll Be a Woman Soon" that appeared on their no-budget 1992 EP *Stull*. The director astutely realized that the song would provide the perfect tone to a scene involving the early moments of Vincent Vega (John Travolta) and Mia Wallace (Uma Thurman), the sexy, seductive calm before a druggy shit storm.

Characteristically protective of his songs, Diamond's representatives apparently passed initially on clearing "Girl, You'll Be a Woman Soon" for use in the picture, a decision that would reverse with exceedingly positive results for all involved. Diamond's back catalog got a major boost, moving many more units of all his past albums and anthologies. Among its many other achievements, *Pulp Fiction* succeeded in introducing a newer, younger crowd to the sultry feel of Neil.

For all that good news, 1994 was also clearly among the worst of times on a profoundly personal level. After nearly twenty-five years of marriage, his wife, Marcia, filed for divorce in October 1994, making him a solitary man once again.

When asked about his second divorce, Diamond, true to form, made no excuses. "I think I'm a very difficult person to be with and to live with. I don't know how these amazing women that I was married to were able to do it."

In time, the split between Neil and Marcia Diamond would become legend among celebrity divorce obsessives, with the reported $150 million settlement often getting at or near the top of the charts for those who keep score of such things.

Rather than sit around Los Angeles feeling sorry for himself, Diamond opted to play a different tune. Badly in need of a change of scenery, Neil left his usual Los Angeles haunts to write and record in Nashville. He had been urged to try recording in Music City by his longtime producer and friend Bob Gaudio, who had lived and worked there happily. Nashville was also home to a number of Diamond's friends, like former guitarist Richard Bennett and one of country's greatest outlaws, Waylon Jennings.

Certainly something in the plaintive sound of country music suited the heartbreak that Diamond and his family were now experiencing. As Neil explained, "I think that going to Nashville was getting away, running away from a terrible emotional situation, and going to a place that I felt that was friendly, and would be friendly and *was* friendly."

As a legendary songwriter beloved and respected in numerous genres, Diamond didn't have to look hard to make friends. He moved to Nashville in 1994 and spent months mixing things up with many of the town's best songwriters, from the legendary Harlan Howard, with whom he wrote "Blue Highway," to far younger talents like Raul Malo of the Mavericks, with whom he penned "Reminisce for a While." Diamond and Gaudio then recorded in Nashville with many of the town's first-call session aces, as well as some members of Diamond's touring group. The resulting album is proof positive that such a collaborative process in Music City need not lead to generic tunesmithing. Indeed,

Diamond's writing sounded intensely personal, even though the only track he had written by himself was the even more countrified remake of "Kentucky Woman."

Nashville's warmth toward Diamond, and Diamond's warmth right back, was very much on display in *Neil Diamond: Under a Tennessee Moon*, an ABC prime-time special featuring Diamond performing at the intimate and historic Ryman Auditorium, the mother church of country music. In the special Diamond spoke of how his early time in Cheyenne, Wyoming, had helped shape him. "I became infatuated with cowboys and cowboy singers, and guitars—all of that Western stuff when we lived there," he explained. "I think I've always been interested in country music." In particular, he spoke of his love of the Everly Brothers, who moved so comfortably from country music to rock and roll, and of Chet Atkins as being an early guitar hero.

In the ABC special, Chet Atkins would join Diamond, as on the album, to perform "Blue Highway" after Diamond introduced him as "the sexiest seventy-year-old guitar player in the world." "Blue Highway," like "Tennessee Moon," was an affecting song about escape, a theme with which Diamond had no trouble connecting. Discussing the title song he would write with Dennis Morgan, Diamond said that he liked the image of a Tennessee moon and the spell it would cast: "It became my story." Bill LaBounty, with whom Diamond cowrote my personal favorite album cut, "Can Anybody Hear Me," appeared on the show and shared one insight on what it's like to write a song with Neil Diamond. "The guy doesn't write a song," LaBounty explained. "He sort of *wills* a song."

On *Tennessee Moon*, Diamond had willed himself back to peak form. The album was not simply a successful crossover move from a pop superstar, it was one of the stronger contemporary country albums of its era, and Diamond's best effort since *Beautiful Noise*.

Another highlight of *Tennessee Moon* was Diamond's duet with his old friend Waylon Jennings on "One Good Love," a romantic ballad Neil wrote with Gary Nicholson. In the ABC special, Jennings explained that he had long assumed that Diamond was from Los Angeles originally, and thus dubbed him "Hollywood Hillbilly," which he apparently meant as a compliment. "One Good Love," Diamond said, was inspired by Jennings' relationship with his wife, Jessie Colter, whom Diamond explained Jennings was always "braggin' on." Listening to "One Good Love" now, one wishes that Diamond had been drafted by Jennings to join the Highwaymen with Johnny Cash, Willie Nelson, and Kris Kristofferson. Beyond being a great track, "One Good Love" is more than a duet, it's a sort of summit meeting of two great deep voices.

The surprisingly funny "Talking Optimist Blues" directly addressed fears of being "overtaxed and alimonied / tired of eatin' fried baloney," but ultimately reaffirmed Diamond's desire to overcome his fears. Still, the inclusion of a very pretty love song called "Marry Me," sung as a duet with a young singer named Buffy Lawson, seemed like extremely curious timing. Far better was "Everybody," a far deeper and more universal sort of love song that Diamond wrote with someone he loved dearly, his son, Jesse. Diamond has said that there was "great meaning and satisfaction" in the process of writing with one of his children. Though not terribly country sounding, "Everybody" was simply stunning, and he performed the delicate gem powerfully at the Ryman with the help of Richard Bennett on guitar and master fiddle player Mark O'Connor.

Neil Diamond: Under a Tennessee Moon concluded with an all-star version of "Kentucky Woman" with Diamond joined onstage by Tim McGraw, Hal Ketchum, Raul Malo, and Waylon Jennings, more deep-voiced cowboys than you could shake a stick at without getting seriously hurt.

Country superstar Tim McGraw summed things up wonderfully in the special. "I think Neil Diamond when you talk about him, he embraces all kinds of music," McGraw said. "You don't put him in a category. And he touches a lot of people who listen to rap, who listen to country, who listen to rock and roll, who listen to pop. *Everybody* knows who Neil Diamond is. I think the best way to describe American music is with Neil Diamond."

On so many levels, coming to Nashville had worked out well for Neil. Diamond's best album in years went all the way to #3 on the country charts and #14 on the pop charts. Professionally, Neil Diamond was undergoing a remarkable and at times surprising resurgence. His songs continued to appear prominently in movies like *Beautiful Girls* ("Sweet Caroline") and *Donnie Brasco* ("Love on the Rocks") and on TV in hit shows like *Friends* and *The Simpsons*. And Diamond's concerts continued to get bigger than ever. In fact, *Amusement Business* magazine would name him the top solo concert act of the nineties. Some of those many sold-out shows provided the material for Diamond's latest concert album, 1995's *Live in America*. Other vintage performances would appear on *Live in Concert*, a three-CD collection of concert recordings issued as a special release through Reader's Digest.

But if fans new and old were looking for a one-stop spot to satisfy all their Neil Diamond needs, the place to go was *In My Lifetime*, a three-CD retrospective that covered all eras of Diamond's career—Bang, Uni, and Columbia—and featured numerous previously unreleased tracks. This was a box set that did something that has been done too rarely in Diamond's career: it took Neil's body of work seriously and documented it lovingly.

In My Lifetime became much more than a contractual obligation to Diamond, who even wrote a title track for the album as well as opening up his archives as never before. The album featured everything from his earliest recording to his latest work, and came complete with liner notes by me and song-by-song comments from the man himself. As Neil wrote in his introduction, "Listening to this compilation is like having my life pass before my ears: personal moments, aspirations, things I was sure nobody would ever hear, all returning to trigger memories, taking me back to a long time ago." For the record, spending time in Diamond's offices with Sam Cole, Alison Zanetos, and Sherrie Levy working on *In My Lifetime* was one of the more pleasant gigs in my lifetime. Along with a team from Columbia, Diamond built a stellar box set, perhaps knowing that if he built it, they would come. The three CDs in *In My Lifetime* became one of those rare box sets that sold so well that it charted on the *Billboard* top two hundred, hitting #122 and going on to go gold.

Nineteen ninety-nine's *The Movie Album: As Time Goes By,* Neil's last album of the twentieth century, found the singer looking further back in the century for his material. On the album's handsome cover, Diamond is dressed in a tuxedo. Inside he worked his way through some of the greatest and most romantic songs ever to come to us from the silver screen, conducted by the great, Oscar-winning composer Elmer Bernstein, whose own movie scores include *The Ten Commandments, The Man with the Golden Arm, The Magnificent Seven,* and *To Kill a Mockingbird.* Diamond's song choices here ranged from "Moon River" to "Can You Feel the Love Tonight" from *The Lion King.* In his essay for the album, Diamond wrote about Elmer Bernstein, "who fell for my pitch that I could sing these movie classics." Diamond went on to add that he *knew* he could sing this music because he'd been "singing some of them since I was a kid."

Diamond was hardly the first or last pop superstar to record an album of popular standards, and though he would make no one forget

Frank Sinatra, he acquitted himself well, particularly on the title track from *Casablanca* and "Windmills of My Mind," cowritten by his recent "If There Were No Dreams" collaborator, Michel Legrand.

All things considered, *The Movie Album: As Time Goes By* performed well, especially for a double-CD set, reaching #31, and even scored a Grammy nomination for best traditional pop vocal performance. At the Forty-second Annual Grammy Awards, Diamond ultimately lost to Tony Bennett, which likely cushioned the blow a bit.

For what it was worth, Neil Diamond had proved that he could sing the American songbook. In the century ahead, Neil would do something much more impressive and meaningful: he would write his own classic songs and once again live up to his own very highest standards with his own still-expanding songbook.

Song Sung 12

HELL YEAH

Been around a good long while
So I gotta say it fast
Time is all we'll ever need
But it's gotta have a meaning
You be careful how it's spent
Cause it isn't going to last

—"HELL YEAH," BY NEIL DIAMOND

HE AIN'T HEAVY . . . HE'S NEIL DIAMOND.

That said, right at the start of the twenty-first century, a weighty responsibility, and a real honor, fell from the skies like some particularly heavy lead *kreplach* upon my chubby yet still strangely narrow shoulders.

Sometime in 2000, I got a phone call from Neil's then longtime publicist, the always warm and wonderful Sherrie Levy, informing me that Neil Diamond would agree to participate in an episode of the then popular VH1 series *Behind the Music* to promote his next album if I produced the hour-long show. This may have just been some nice way to stroke my considerable ego, but much like the next smug bastard, I'll take my celebrity ego strokes wherever I can get them.

This request was not exactly out of the blue. By then I had been involved for years in a number of capacities with *Behind the Music*, the popular and, let it be said, highly entertaining cable TV series. I had been associated with the show both on camera, as one of those self-satisfied cultural commentators waxing semieloquent as if on cue, and off camera, working behind the scenes as a producer, writer, and interviewer on a number of episodes.

Almost immediately, I confronted the reality that attempting to produce an episode of *Behind the Music* about Neil Diamond would present its own very particular and peculiar series of inherent challenges. First, I realized that telling a long and illustrious life story like Neil's in only a single hour of television with any level of depth or insight would not prove an easy task. Unlike some one- or two-hit wonder, there was a lot of career to document here. Indeed, covering a substantial and worthwhile musical life story like Neil Diamond's would probably take an entire loving and self-indulgent book like, well, almost *exactly* like this one.

That, however, was not the built-in challenge to this gig that *really* worried me at the time. No, what scared the hell out of me here was the issue of exactly what kind of story we would be telling about Neil Diamond, one that was to a large degree actually *about* the music. As a general and well-established rule, *Behind the Music* was, true to its name, less about the music itself and *much* more about all those assorted acts of bad behavior—backstabbings and blow jobs—that so often seem to occur behind, in front of, and just about anywhere in the general vicinity of our popular musicians.

And so it came to pass that *Behind the Music* tended not to be, first and foremost, television with really good taste, but rather TV that *tasted* good. At its best, *Behind the Music* was a real pleasure. At its worst, *Behind the Music* was a real guilty pleasure. Years before *Us*

Weekly and TMZ successfully transformed a constant procession of celebrity screwups into a major media growth industry, *Behind the Music* founded a similar formula in the music world, one that for better or worse seemed to work exceedingly well. Basically, that winning formula all came down to this single core equation: rock stars plus bad behavior equals good TV.

The part about rock stars was all fine and well, but the part about bad behavior was, for all intents and purposes, downright mandatory. Indeed, some of the most popular and buzzed-about episodes of the *Behind the Music* series concentrated on such notable "musicians" as teen-dream-turned-adult-nightmare Leif Garrett and those infamous lip-synching legends Milli Vanilli. For the record, I put those quote marks around the word musician not to be snide, but simply to stop myself from throwing up as I typed the sentence. With all due respect, which is to say none, Leif Garrett and Milli Vanilli were on an artistic level hardly worthy of being considered as Neil Diamond's roadies, much less his "musical" colleagues.

As a serious-minded, important American artist who's largely behaved himself for decades at a time as far as we know, Neil Diamond was, shall we say, a far less obvious fit with this sort of TV show. Furthermore, as a surprisingly private man for such an enduring public figure, Neil simply didn't seem to fit the highly predictable, extremely comforting *Behind the Music* story arc: a very quick rise followed quickly by a very hard fall, a few big hits playing as the soundtrack to a series of shocking overdoses or other public displays of human wreckage. I had to wonder, was Neil Diamond's story in a sense way too good to tell here?

Ultimately, I decided that it was worth attempting to bring the world a *Behind the Music* show about Neil that actually was primarily about the music itself, and some very good music at that. I had two reasons. First of all, at least relatively speaking, this felt like a reasonably noble cause. Second, they were paying me. And so along with the rest of our splendid and dedicated little *Behind the Music* team, I would attempt to thread the needle and help make an episode that would be entertaining while also allowing Neil to maintain the dignity that has always been one of his many precious possessions.

Despite all my fears, Neil's *Behind the Music* show turned out to be a pleasure to work on in part because once he decides to participate in something, Neil Diamond maintains the power to open up a lot of doors. More than any other artist I've ever known, Neil seems to own and control his creative work. Calling upon that power on our behalf, Neil generously opened up much of his life to our production team. Along with his own great team, including Sherrie Levy, Sam Cole, and Alison Zanetos, Neil made our jobs infinitely easier by providing us with excellent footage and photos, as well as an interview that was unusually candid from a man who's wise enough to be far more careful than your average celebrity with their mouth open.

At my own somewhat nervy request, Neil even managed to dig up his failed Lenny Bruce screen test so that we could show a little clip of it in the show. And as if all that wasn't enough, Neil performed a couple of his most popular songs on camera in his recording studio just for us to weave into the musical and visual fabric of our show, gratis. Standing there with Neil in his natural environment and having him play a few of our requests was the sort of "job" for which I believe many of us reading this would gladly pay dearly.

And so, yes, Virginia, once upon a time there really was a *Behind the Music* that could actually have been called *About the Music*. Even without the sort of embarrassing acts of self-destruction that seemed to be mandatory on the series, the Neil Diamond episode performed well enough in the TV ratings, which proved one of two things: (1) the remarkable dedication of Diamond's fan base or (2) the willingness of *Behind the Music* sin-seeking fans to wait until the bitter end of any given episode in desperate hopes of some last-minute breakdown, OD, or sudden sex addiction.

In retrospect, perhaps it was really both things. After all, pop culture history suggests two things: hope does spring eternal and Diamond fans are forever.

Working on Neil's *Behind the Music* was another powerful reminder of just how splendid the man's music was, and thankfully that was not only speaking in the distant past tense. I remember being invited to go into Neil's office sometime in early 2001 to hear the new album Neil wanted to promote by doing *Behind the Music*. Neil and his longtime musical associate Sam Cole put me in the studio, darkened the lights, and let me hear the wonderfully titled and extremely encouraging *Three Chord Opera*. For me at least, this sometimes undervalued album represented another crucial, sometimes overlooked step that helped set the stage for Neil's even greater twenty-first century triumphs still to come.

Recording in the aftermath of some serious emotional upheaval, Neil's previous studio album, *Tennessee Moon,* had found Diamond drawing upon the power of Music City USA to refocus his own long-standing passion for songwriting. Something about the familiar yet new experience of working with many of the finest tunesmiths from Music City seemed to revive Diamond's own sense of songcraft. It was almost as if the exposure to Nashville's competitive but close-knit community somehow brought him back to his early days trying to find his path on New York's Tin Pan Alley. And as if now repeating a much earlier pattern, Diamond's next studio album would find him going his own way again in a sense, as he eventually returned to Los Angeles to record *Three Chord Opera*, remarkably his very first album of songs written entirely by himself since the *Serenade* album way back in 1974.

Diamond himself also seemed very aware that his remarkable recent renewal as a songwriter was in fact a gradual process. As he explained to Steve Baltic in a 2008 interview that appeared online on Spinner.com, "I started really with the *Tennessee Moon* album, co-writing all the songs. It was intentional to work with a lot of different writers in Nashville. I had a lot of fun. That started to get the barnacles and rust off of my writing chops. Then, *Three Chord Opera* was maybe all mine. That continued that process of the rust falling off."

Two thousand and one's *Three Chord Opera*, produced by Peter Asher and Alan Lindgren, stands as another important step in this artistic rust-removal process, another turning point on the way to Diamond's remarkable revival that would follow, as well as a very fine album in its own right. However, Neil's effort to compose his *Three Chord Opera* would prove slightly operatic, as following *Tennessee Moon* Diamond encountered a bad brush with writer's block, a hardly uncommon affliction among artists to which Neil previously had been largely immune.

The solution to Diamond's worrying writer's block problem arrived in a most unusual and highly amusing form. In 2000, Diamond was approached with the sort of offer that apparently not even he could refuse, and he refuses many of them. The offer came from the makers of a new film comedy called *Saving Silverman*, concerning the exploits of a group of buddies who play together in a scruffy Neil Diamond tribute band called Diamonds in the Rough. Wisely, the filmmakers offered Diamond a small but important cameo in the movie. Neil was to play the part of Neil Diamond, truly the role of a lifetime.

In this youth-oriented comedy, Diamond would appear alongside a talented cast that included Jack Black, Steve Zahn, Jason Biggs, and

Amanda Peet. The director was Dennis Dugan, whose previous credits included the extremely popular and amusing Adam Sandler box-office hits *Happy Gilmore* and *Big Daddy*. As if that wasn't enough, the offer to write a song for the *Saving Silverman* end credits inspired Diamond to write a new song called "I Believe in Happy Endings," an uplifting number that much like "Song Sung Blue" had a certain charmingly profound simplicity as both a song and a personal statement.

In our *Behind the Music* episode, Peter Asher told me that having to write this movie song to order, "Brill Building style," as he quite rightly put it, seemed to force Diamond back into his creative zone as a songwriter. Fortunately, once back in the zone, the writing block was broken and the floodgates opened. As Neil explained to me in that same show, "Doing this music for the movie opened up whatever the clogged valves of my creative mind were, and showed me that I *could* do it, and that was all I needed."

And so *Three Chord Opera* became the sound of those floodgates opening. The album's wild opening track, "I Haven't Played That Song in Years," was one of Diamond's deeply personal explorations of his past and present, and a song that sounded like some lost and now found classic from the past. Stripped of its big orchestra arrangement, "I Haven't Played That Song in Years" can be heard to point the way toward the remarkable albums that would follow. Other highlights here ranged from the upbeat love song "You're the Best Part of Me" to the dramatic "Midnight Dream" and "Elijah's Song," a lovely salute to Neil's new grandchild by son, Jesse, and his actress wife, Sheryl Lee.

Considering the now somewhat reduced commercial expectations, *Three Chord Opera* performed fairly well on the charts, peaking at #15 on the *Billboard* two hundred, and #2 on the top Internet album charts, while the extremely accessible "You're the Best Part of Me" would become a top-thirty adult contemporary hit. Still, as was the case with *Saving Silverman* when it came out in 2001, the reviewers weren't always kind. Roger Ebert managed to put down both Neil and the movie when he wrote, "As for Neil Diamond, *Saving Silverman* is his first appearance in a fiction film since *The Jazz Singer* (1980), and one can only marvel that he waited 20 years to appear in a second film, and found one even worse than his first one." As I saw it, *Saving Silverman* may not have been *Citizen Kane*, or even *Car Wash*, but it certainly had its charms, Diamond among them.

As for *Three Chord Opera*, the usually astute Bill Crandall wrote a decidedly mixed album review in *Rolling Stone* that ended by damning the album with the following faint praise: "But, hey, my mom will dig it." In this case at least, Bill's mother knew better.

Fortunately, Mrs. Crandall wasn't the only one appreciating Neil in the early days of the new century. In the summer of 2000, Diamond received a rare second honor from the Songwriters Hall of Fame into which he had already been inducted. Diamond was awarded the prestigious Sammy Cahn Lifetime Achievement Award at a ceremony in New York. To a man who had often thought of himself first and foremost as a songwriter, this honor must have been especially meaningful, particularly having spent so many years trying to find his place in Tin Pan Alley.

In 2001, the first number one hit that Diamond ever wrote, "I'm a Believer," became a sizable hit yet again when the California band Smash Mouth recorded the song in a slightly punkier rendition that appeared prominently in the animated smash *Shrek*. Diamond would later reward Smash Mouth by giving them a more newly minted pop gem he wrote called "You Are My Number One" for their next album. This song didn't get to number one, but it was encouraging to veteran Diamondheads that Neil was now sufficiently back in the writer's groove to start giving good songs away.

At this point, Diamond had good and deeply personal reasons to be writing more love songs all of a sudden. By now he had a new woman in his life: Rae Fawley, a very attractive, considerably younger Australian marketing executive with whom he remains very happily involved to this day. In 2008, Diamond agreed to participate in the Dear Superstar section of the music magazine *Blender*, in which fans send in questions to be answered by some legend. Someone with an inquisitive mind from La Crosse, Wisconsin, had the following query: "OK, Mr. Ladies' Man: What's the secret to dating a woman who's half your age?" Diamond handled the question extremely well. "Chemistry," he explained. "And I don't mean Viagra. I believe it's the same whether she's half your age or twice your age. People either connect or they don't."

Sadly, there was inevitably some heartbreak along the way too, including the sudden passing in June of 2001 of longtime Neil Diamond band member Vince Charles. When he returned to the road later in 2001, Diamond would add "Captain Sunshine" from his 1972 album *Moods* as a moving salute to the man on steel drums with the great smile who had brought so much to his music for so long. By that time, however, Neil's tour would begin in the wake of an utterly unimaginable human tragedy.

Just weeks after September 11, Neil Diamond set off on his 2001–2002 concert tour. Before concluding on New Year's Eve 2002, Diamond and the band would play 120 shows in ninety cities. As he would later recount in his revealing liner notes essay for the *12 Songs* album, these shows took on greater meaning and "quickly evolved into something bigger than just a tour." Based on the homecoming concert stop that I saw in Los Angeles, this was the most powerful, intense, and emotional show of Neil Diamond's career.

Especially in that context, it was entirely understandable that Neil left the 2001–2002 tour thinking that in 2003 all he really wanted to do was, as he wrote in his *12 Songs* essay, "rest, relax and sit outside with the sun on my face doing as little work as possible."

Fortunately for Diamond fans, that sort of time off was simply not in the cards. Instead, in January 2003, Neil found himself in his cabin in the Rockies writing songs as a blizzard raged outside. That first writing session in the storm would lead into the beginning of a beautiful and important new creative relationship in Diamond's life.

Neil heard that Rick Rubin, arguably the single hippest and most in-demand producer in the world, was extremely interested in producing him. Rubin had first made his name working with the likes of Run DMC and the Beastie Boys, going on to produce everyone from Slayer to the Dixie Chicks, Danzig to Donovan, including the Red Hot Chili Peppers, Tom Petty, and Mick Jagger, as well as a stunning series album for Johnny Cash, the *American Recordings* that allowed the Man in Black to go out very much on top. One imagines that Diamond had to be impressed by the fact that Rubin had by now already produced Johnny Cash's Grammy-winning version of "Solitary Man," a characteristically excellent, stripped-down recording of Diamond's classic song. It featured Tom Petty on backing vocals and became the title track of Rubin's third album with Cash, 2000's *American III: Solitary Man*.

Even with all that, by this point in his long and distinguished career, Diamond did not rush to work with *anyone*, even Rick Rubin. As Diamond explained to Sylvie Simmons in a 2008 interview with the British music magazine *Mojo*, "Well this was a leap of faith for me, because I didn't know Rick and I'm very picky with producers, I've worked with the best producers in the business."

Yet Neil Diamond had never worked with a producer quite like Rick Rubin, each of these two men being very much one of a kind. In one superficial sense, Diamond and Rubin might have seemed an artistic odd couple to those who still defined Rubin based on his early groundbreaking work in rap and his love of heavy metal. It was Rubin, for instance, who had helped bring the world the fusion of rap and rock by producing Run DMC and Aerosmith's collaboration on their influential reworking of that latter group's "Walk This Way."

In another sense, however, the match of Diamond and Rubin made considerable sense. After all, Rubin was, like me, a Jewish kid who had grown up in the New York area in the late sixties and seventies, happily hearing Neil Diamond's music everywhere on the airwaves. When I recently asked Rubin about his first memories of Diamond's music, he explained, "Growing up, Neil's music was ubiquitous. 'Solitary Man' and 'Girl, You'll Be a Woman Soon' are the songs I can remember as early standouts."

When asked what he responded to in Diamond's early music, Rubin, a music executive as well as a producer, further demonstrated his eye for talent. "He doesn't sound like anyone else," Rubin told me. "He writes very specific deep moody songs, often having an operatic arc. Great, unique melodies and great guitar rhythms. Oh yes, he sings really well, too!"

Indeed, Diamond does sing very well, to the point where for many other singers recording some of the man's most familiar songs might seem like risky business. Sometimes, however, that risk pays off in a big way, such as when Johnny Cash brought his own deep-voiced, solitary persona to his rendition of Diamond's classic "Solitary Man."

It had been Rubin's smart suggestion that Cash record "Solitary Man," but Rubin tells me he is uncertain exactly what role the track had in furthering his working relationship with the song's writer and original singer. "I played the song for Johnny and he was excited to record it," Rubin recalls. "Don't know if it had anything to do with us getting together."

Diamond and Rubin getting together would be a gradual process that first involved sitting down and talking music. Before long they were connected through their shared overriding passion. Eventually, the pair got down to work, recording what Diamond at first considered demos, but would eventually realize were a very different sort of Neil Diamond recordings. For the first time in a long while, Diamond not only sang but played guitar on these remarkable new tracks. Rubin used Diamond's voice and guitar playing as the core of recordings that revealed Diamond's old strengths in a new light: "The goal was to make the best album we could, reflecting where Neil was at that moment in his life. Personal, intimate, honest."

Eventually, two excellent guitarists would bring their talents to *12 Songs* as well: Mike Campbell of Tom Petty and the Heartbreakers fame and Smokey Hormel, best known for his work with Beck. Other outstanding musicians added subtle but important parts, including Billy Preston, the Heartbreakers' Benmont Tench, and session great Larry Knechtel on assorted keyboards. Yet the fact that Diamond was playing guitar himself helped bring the album a sort of intimacy and original passion that had too often been missing from Diamond's later recordings.

"Neil played guitar during our preproduction sessions and it was clear his playing was the best indicator of the rhythm and feel of the track," Rubin recalled to me. "He was apprehensive about playing guitar as he felt there were much better guitar players than he was, but what was needed wasn't virtuoso playing, it was the ability to get the song over and no one would do that as well as Neil."

Rubin was perhaps most impressed by Diamond's extraordinary work ethic. "He may work harder than any artist I've seen before, and is very hard on himself," Rubin told me. "Saying he's driven doesn't come close; maybe 'devoted' would be a good word."

Because of such devotion, *12 Songs* took time to get right. As Diamond wrote in his essay on the album, "Rick was determined not to rush the process, but to wait until we got to the essence of the songs I was working on."

As a result, there was no new Neil Diamond album between 2001's *Three Chord Opera* and the eventual release of *12 Songs* in 2005.

In the years between studio albums, Diamond's name continued to be out there, thanks in part to numerous rereleases and archival releases, including 2001's *The Essential Neil Diamond,* 2002's *Love Songs,* and the most complete collection yet of Diamond's Uni work, *Play Me: The Complete Uni Studio Recordings—Plus!* The year 2003 then saw the release of the biggest box yet: *Stages: Performances 1970–2002,* a massive collection of concert performances gathered on five CDs and one DVD.

As Diamond continued to work away on *12 Songs* with Rubin, he took a little time out for one amazing night in the summer of 2004. I happened to be writing speeches for two major, star-studded fund-raisers for Democratic presidential candidate John Kerry when I heard some exciting news. Neil had agreed not only to appear at the Los Angeles event being held at the new Walt Disney Concert Hall, but also to once again take the stage and sing "You Don't Bring Me Flowers" with a prominent Democratic voice by the name of Barbra Streisand. Watching these two former Erasmus High schoolmates rehearse together after all these years was a lot more fun than any high school reunion I ever attended.

That night's show, which host Billy Crystal described as Woodstock "for really, really rich people," had many highlights, with appearances by the likes of Leonardo DiCaprio, Ben Affleck, and many others. For me, however, the heart of the show came after Ben Stiller introduced Neil by thanking him for being "the man who helped me get to second base for the first time in my life" during a date to see *The Jazz Singer* and for being "my personal savior in a very rocky adolescence."

Neil sang "Forever in Blue Jeans," "Sweet Caroline," and of course "America," as well as sharing "You Don't Bring Me Flowers" with Streisand one more time.

Okay, so we may have lost the presidential election and in the process allowed the single most disastrous second term in history to take place, yet for one night at least, everyone in Disney Hall felt like big winners.

When it was finally released in late 2005, *12 Songs* was a work that reflected Diamond's devotion in the best way, and for once, such obvious artistic excellence was duly noted by much of the world media. *Newsweek* dubbed *12 Songs* as "the best work Diamond has done in 30 years." England's *Q* magazine, meanwhile, was even more effusive in their praise. "It may well be his best record ever," they proclaimed.

Asked what lesson could be learned from the way *12 Songs* restored Diamond's reputation as a great American artist in his own right, "Really good work is recognized," Rick Rubin told me. "It always counts. We have seen other examples of grown-up artists having success by pandering to the marketplace or to the current styles, fads or sounds. What's interesting about *12 Songs* is it's an album of new material recorded with NO DRUMS and it's not an album full of duets with all of the 'flavors of the month.' It's a pure, serious Neil Diamond album, not a marketing-driven 'event' album. It's refreshing."

Initially, at least, the public responded with equal excitement to Diamond's refreshing new musical statement. Then out of the blue, as if in some corporate Greek tragedy, idiocy struck. While *12 Songs* debuted impressively on the *Billboard* chart at #4, almost immediately word started to spread that Columbia Records had decided to put antipiracy, virus-vulnerable software on the CD that rendered unsuspecting consumers' PCs vulnerable to hacking.

The reaction was instant and devastating. Lawsuits soon followed, as they tend to do, and just as the most acclaimed and important album of Neil Diamond's career started to sell, *12 Songs* was literally recalled from stores, pulled from distribution quicker than some lethal child's toy. Eventually, Diamond's album would be rereleased, but sadly, the damage had already been done.

"It was heartbreaking," Rubin tells me now. "We put two or more years into that album and to see all of that work compromised by a moronic corporate mistake . . ."

Another artist might have taken this blow as some sort of sign that it was time to throw in the digital towel. Fortunately, Neil Diamond is not, and never has been, just another artist.

ENCORE

I Believe in Happy Endings

Free the word from the page
Free the bird from the cage
Just go out there and face what you did before
Did it once, you can do it once more

—"ONE MORE BITE OF THE APPLE," BY NEIL DIAMOND

How can you really end a story about something that you *really* love, something that's not over by any stretch of the imagination?

I have pondered this precise rhetorical question while staring at a blank document on my now overheated and filthy MacBook Pro. I have now come to this temporary final conclusion.

For my money, at least for my book advance money, you really have to finish *big* just as you would in a great romantic comedy or a truly satisfying personal massage—with a happy ending. And as Neil Diamond said in his uplifting song of the same name, I *believe* in happy endings. And, wouldn't you know it, here comes a happy ending right about now.

This book, which you have presumably been reading thus far, is a heartfelt expression of one man's platonic love for the music of another man. Beyond any possible profit motive, and trust me it ain't quite as much of a profit as you might imagine, this book has been written out of a true love of Neil Diamond's music; more specifically, *my* true love of Neil Diamond's music. This Greatest Love of All has endured for virtually all of my life—through albums, eras, and hair styles thick and thin—though, for the record, I myself was never actually thin for any of those albums or eras, and haven't had all that much hair to worry about in years.

So fortunately, absolutely no thanks to me, this book just so happens to conclude during a time that finds its hero not simply alive and well, but to a remarkable degree quite literally at the very top of his game. At an age when many artists take it easy or simply stop, Neil Diamond has gone the other way with magnificent and, yes, exceedingly happy results. For whatever reasons, Diamond has in the twenty-first century become ravenously hungry again, not for commercial success, or even media validation, but instead for true artistic success. Don't call it a comeback, but as I write these final words, having already passed my contractually required word count, Neil Diamond is, creatively speaking, back on top with a vengeance.

The album *12 Songs* had represented a dozen giant steps in the right direction, at least until Neil found himself almost instantly undermined by one woefully misguided or at least clueless act of his own record company. Yet when Columbia's digital shit hit Diamond's fans and destroyed the album's momentum in 2005, the blow ultimately only served to increase our man's determination. Rather than pack up in disgust, Neil Diamond soon got back to work as if with an even deeper desire to right this shocking wrong. Dealing with first things first, a little over a year after the original 2005 release of *12 Songs*, Diamond revisited the album with a special limited-edition 2-CD set that featured the CD *Artist's Cut: 12 Sketches* with alternate takes, and thankfully totally free of any Orwellian doomsday software.

Even better, having done his best to put this spyware mishap behind him, Diamond pushed forward, deciding before too long that he would reteam with Rubin to record another album. Yet there were other changes to be made in his career, perhaps partly to help avoid such disasters in the future.

After managing himself for a number of years, Diamond chose to sign with perhaps the most legendary and powerful new manager around, Irving Azoff. Azoff is an ongoing force of nature in his own right. In addition to his long-standing, historically successful relationship with the Eagles, Azoff currently represents everyone from Christina Aguilera to Van Halen, Steely Dan to New Kids on the Block. As the traditional music business model collapsed in the twenty-first century, Azoff increasingly seemed like one of the only figures able to stay ahead of the curve. Working under Azoff, a young manager named Katie McNeil would bring a new energy and excitement to Team Diamond.

Amazingly, as fate would have it, Diamond would soon end up with an important friend in a very high place at Columbia Records. At the time of the unfortunate *12 Songs* meltdown, "Neil was furious and I vowed never to make another album with Columbia," Rick Rubin told journalist Lynn Hirschberg in a revealing September 2007 profile for *New York Times Magazine*. Ultimately, Rubin found a far better and more surprising way to beat 'em—he joined 'em at an extremely high level. In May of 2007, shortly after winning the producer of the year award at the Grammys, Rubin, Neil's new producer and close musical partner in crime, was named cohead of Columbia, Diamond's longtime recording home. As much as possible, Diamond now had reason to believe that his next triumph would not be undone by an unforeseen outrage like copy protection.

By the time Rubin took his power position at Columbia, he and Diamond were already at work together on the album that would eventually become *Home Before Dark*.

In the spring of 2008, Katie McNeil kindly invited me to the offices of Azoff Music Management to be one of the first people outside of the studio to hear Neil's latest effort, then in the final stages of mixing and mastering. Listening to *Home Before Dark* for the first time that day was one of those moments when I realized how well placed my faith in Neil's music had been all these years. It was also the moment that made me realize that I had a book to get off my chest.

If *12 Songs* was the sound of Neil Diamond trying his best to be a truly great recording artist, *Home Before Dark* is something even more remarkable. This is an inspired and deeply felt song cycle that finds an even more comfortable Diamond simply doing and being his personal best. Even more than *12 Songs*, *Home Before Dark* reflects not simply the Neil Diamond that we thought we once knew, but the man that really exists now. And at age sixty-seven, that is a slightly older and even wiser man who has been around the block a few times, and still passionately wants to stick around long enough for at least, as one outstanding song memorably puts it, "One More Bite of the Apple."

Diamond, as Rubin told me, "felt more confident after the success of *12 Songs* and he brought that with him into the record-making process."

Home Before Dark is to my ears quite possibly the single greatest album of Neil Diamond's entire career thus far. That would be a remarkable achievement anytime but especially at this late date. The old cliché "You're not getting older, you're getting better" does not quite apply. Here Diamond getting older and getting better seem logically connected. Right from the opening intimate epic, "If I Don't See You Again," to the concluding and luminous title track, Neil Diamond is openly exploring matters of love and friendship as if they are matters of life and death, which of course they have always been.

More than ever, the songs feel revealing, whether Neil is writing about love in terms almost religious on the stunning "Pretty Amazing Grace," addressing his own fears of being "Forgotten," or simply offering some solid advice on the sexy and witty "Don't Go There." What a thrill it was to hear Neil Diamond and the Dixie Chicks' Natalie Maines singing a great new song of love lost, with its aching echoes of "I Got the Feelin' (Oh No, No)." How encouraging it was to hear the Solitary Man himself still optimistically extolling "The Power of Two."

Not far beneath the surface on *Home Before Dark*, there is a palpable sense of the big clock ticking and every move now counting. Accordingly, and brilliantly, Diamond makes every note count. This is the sound of a man named Neil Diamond literally playing for time, and an album meaningful enough that it makes one dearly hope there will be many more to come.

Yet even if *Home Before Dark* were the last album that Neil Diamond ever recorded, or the last CD ever released, based on the way the music industry is headed toward the trash heap of history, then at least we would be going out with a very big bang.

Some of the media that now started rushing to jump on Neil's bandwagon acted as if Rick Rubin had single-handedly rescued Neil Diamond from his own glittery persona, but that is to suggest far too passive a role for a man as driven as Neil Diamond.

Instead, as he did for Johnny Cash, Rubin seemed to have the excellent taste to simply allow Diamond the musical space to be himself. Rubin looked at the international superstar that Neil Diamond had become and recognized that at the heart of this phenomenon, there was one great American singer-songwriter waiting for a fair hearing. And because of that insight, Rubin gave Diamond the space to once again pick up his guitar, raise his voice, and say his piece.

It says something that having followed Neil Diamond's music so closely for so long, and having known him a bit personally for twenty years now, I feel as though I understand him far better having heard *Home Before Dark* and taken it to heart myself.

As Neil's essay on the *Home Before Dark* album made vividly clear, this was no easy achievement. "Somehow, each album means as much as my very first record, if not more, and the experience of creation has yet to become easy," he revealed. "In truth, I'm as hungry as I ever was: the 'emptiness deep inside' aches even more."

That ache has turned out to be a universal one: in America, *Home Before Dark* entered the *Billboard* album charts at #1, remarkably Neil Diamond's first album to ever reach that zenith. The album would also hit #1 in the United Kingdom and New Zealand and prove popular all around the world.

I asked Rick Rubin what it meant to him to help Neil Diamond to be more fully appreciated, and perhaps to even more fully appreciate himself. "It's a great feeling to see Neil get the recognition as a singer-songwriter, not only a performer," he answered.

More than ever before, this great singer-songwriter and performer too long dismissed as easy listening was telling us the hard truth, in his own words, and in his own songs too.

More than ever before, *Home Before Dark* made me hope that this artistic surge was not just a final victory lap, but a third or fourth shot at a Second Coming.

More than ever before, Diamond's words made me hope that he will write his own book about his music and the singular life to which it is now inextricably tied.

In the meantime, here is mine.

THANK THE LORD
FOR THE NIGHT TIME

In addition to the Lord, I would like to thank the following human beings: my editor Ben Schafer, my literary agent Sarah Lazin, David Steinberger, Irving Azoff, Katie McNeil, Rick Rubin, Jon Rosner, Sherrie Levy, Sam Cole, Alison Zanetos, David Edelstein, Christine Marra, David Gorman, Cameron Crowe, Judd Apatow, Chris Isaak, Jann Wenner and everyone at *Rolling Stone*, as well as Tom Calderone, Lee Rolontz, Rick Krim and everybody at VH1.

Finally, thanks to Neil Diamond himself, for always being a musical god and a real *mensch* too. They say you should never meet your childhood heroes. They are wrong.